SCROLL SAW WORKBOOK

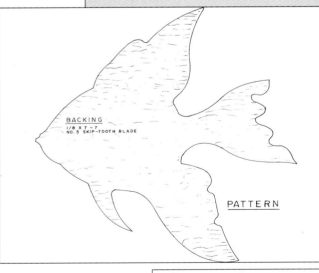

BACKING
1/8 X 7 – 7
NO. 5 SKIP-TOOTH BLADE

PATTERN

by John and Joyce Nelson

Publisher: Alan Giagnocavo
Project Editor: Ayleen Stellhorn
Desktop Specialist: Linda L. Eberly, Eberly Designs Inc.
Interior Photography: Carl Shuman, Owl Hill Studios/Deborah Porter Hayes
Cover Photography: Carl Shuman, Owl Hill Studios

ISBN # 1–56523–207–0

To order your copy of this book,
please send check or money order
for $14.95 plus $2.50 shipping to:
Fox Books
1970 Broad Street
East Petersburg, PA 17520

Printed in China
1 3 5 7 9 10 8 6 4 2

TABLE OF CONTENTS

PREFACE

NOTES FROM THE AUTHORS

Welcome to the world of scrolling. Joyce and I think you will find scrolling rewarding, relaxing and just plain FUN!

Whether you're just beginning or have had some experience with scrolling, you will find something in this book that will help you enjoy scrolling even more than you do now.

This book is based on our eight years of teaching basic and advanced scroll saw classes throughout New England and across the country. Each time we teach a class, we learn something new ourselves, and we would like to pass all we have learned on to you, the reader of this book.

The work sheets and information in this book are based on and follow the classes we have taught. Both Joyce and I want to make it known at the outset that we do not consider ourselves experts on scrolling, so please do not consider us such. We are just passing on what knowledge we do know. We plan to learn much more about scrolling before we are done. We believe in the saying, "You learn something new everyday!" In fact, we have found in our travels that we can learn a lot just meeting and talking with people.

If you can cut out a simple project such as a teddy bear, you can cut out a larger project like our

"Chimes of Joy" clock. Both use the same basic scroll saw techniques. The only difference is that the clock requires more cuts.

We want to thank Dan O'Rourke of Dublin, New Hampshire, for testing and doing all the worksheet projects in this book (Dan had never used a scroll saw before. His finished works are featured in the exercises.); Deborah Porter Hayes of Hancock, New Hampshire, for taking all the photos; and Francis McKenna owner of *Fine Woodworking,* Dublin, New Hampshire, for lending us use of his workshop/showroom to take the photographs.

Last, but not least, we would like to thank Alan Giagnocavo and the staff at Fox Chapel Publishing Company, Inc. Without their help and input this book could not have been published.

It is our sincere hope that *Scroll Saw Workbook* will open up a whole new world of scrolling to you.

Please, feel free to drop Fox Chapel a note if you have any questions, suggestions or criticisms. We would love to hear from you.

Happy Scrolling!

John A. Nelson
Joyce C. Nelson
Dublin, New Hampshire

HOW TO USE THIS WORKBOOK

The first part of this book comprises a variety of information about scroll saws. If you are unfamiliar with the history of scroll saws, you'll want to read through the "History of Scrolling." For an introduction to the scroll saws that are currently on the market, see "Today's Scroll Saws." We've also included information about blades, accessories and materials that can be used with scroll saws.

The hands-on part of this book begins on page 28 with "Getting Started." Be sure to read through this section before you continue with the exercises.

Each exercise has an "Objective." The objective explains what we want you to learn in this exercise. Note each objective before starting, so you will know exactly what you will be doing in each exercise.

After studying the exercise, select and prepare the wood and or materials needed for the exercise. Follow each step in the exercise in the order given.

When completed, compare your finished exercise with the "objective." If you are not completely satisfied with the results or do not feel completely competent in this particular exercise, re-do the entire exercise. It is important that you understand and can execute each exercise before you proceed to the next exercise.

At the end of this book you'll find an appendix listing a number of scroll saw-related suppliers.

THE HISTORY OF SCROLLING

Most people think scrolling started back in 1974 when Helmut Abel of West Germany was granted an International patent for a "new" scroll saw. Some people think scrolling began when Advanced Machinery Imports, Ltd. (A.M.I) of New Castle, Delaware, introduced the Hegner scroll saw to America. Others trace scroll sawing's origins back to 1986 when Patrick Spielman published his wonderful book, *Scroll Saw Handbook.*

In fact, scrolling didn't start with any of these — it all really started way back in the 1500s or so. The very first thin scroll saw blades were made by an early German clockmaker.

I read some time ago that the first person actually associated with

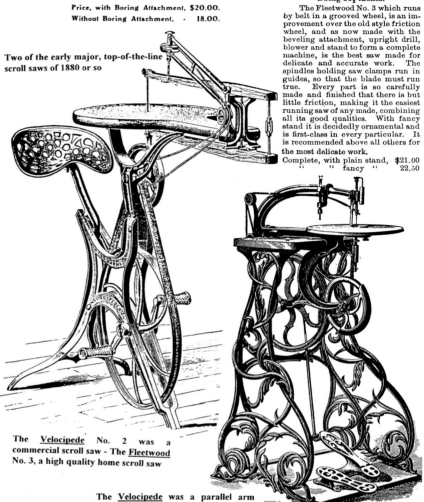

Velocipede Scroll Saw, No. 2.
Price, with Boring Attachment, $20.00.
Without Boring Attachment, - 18.00.

Two of the early major, top-of-the-line scroll saws of 1880 or so

FLEETWOOD No. 3.
Swing 14½ inches.
The Fleetwood No. 3 which runs by belt in a grooved wheel, is an improvement over the old style friction wheel, and as now made with the beveling attachment, upright drill, blower and stand to form a complete machine, is the best saw made for delicate and accurate work. The spindles holding saw clamps run in guides, so that the blade must run true. Every part is so carefully made and finished that there is but little friction, making it the easiest running saw of any made, combining all its good qualities. With fancy stand it is decidedly ornamental and is first-class in every particular. It is recommended above all others for the most delicate work.
Complete, with plain stand, $21.00
"   "   fancy   "   22.50

The <u>Velocipede</u> No. 2 was a commercial scroll saw - The <u>Fleetwood</u> No. 3, a high quality home scroll saw

The <u>Velocipede</u> was a parallel arm saw, the <u>Fleetwood</u>, a rigid arm saw

scrolling was Andre Boulle of Paris, France, in or around 1775. Today there is a famous woodworking school in Paris that is still using Boulle's name.

From 1850 to 1920 scroll sawing in America was as popular as it is today. Many women and children did scrolling back then to supplement the household income, much as we do today.

During those years, there were many companies supplying patterns for the scroll saw, just as today. H.L. Wild of New York City was one of the biggest scroll saw pattern suppliers of the day (from 1880 to 1920). Many of these wonderful, original patterns are being sold today by myself and other scroll saw pattern suppliers.

Many of the patterns in some of my scroll saw books are re-designs of these original project

NEW ROGERS.

Swing between Saw and Frame, 17½ inches.

The Rogers is well finished in all its parts, and will give the most satisfaction of any treadle machine of its price.

Tilting table, drilling attachment and blower, together with three drill points, six saw blades, and a sheet of designs.

No. 1, Japanned table, no emery wheel, $3.50
No. 2, Nickel table, solid emery wheel, 4.00

No. 7 Scroll Saw, Improved.

Price, $15.00.

One of the most popular home scroll saws from 1880 or so — cost $4.00- complete with drilling attachment (Sears also sold a stripped down version of this saw -- less grinding wheel, drilling attachment and quick dis-connect

Both saws use the parallel arm mechanism

The Barnes No. 7 scroll saw was one of the very first scroll saws

patterns. I have tried to record these wonderful original patterns for all times. Large clock patterns we love today, such as the Chimes of Normandy, were sold back then, too.

In 1935 Delta came out with a heavy cast iron, rigid-arm "jig saw." Those of you who grew up

Sample page of full-size scroll saw patterns from Miller Falls Co. of New York

in the forties and fifties, as I did, must remember the big green or gray jig saw in every "manual arts" (woodworking) class. These saws had a true, up-and-down blade motion, but as I remember, left a very rough edge. We spent more time sanding the edges of what we cut than we did cutting out the piece itself.

It was this wonderful new "improved" jig saw that brought scrolling back to America in the forties and early fifties.

As a kid, I remember everyone was making wooden things with this saw. I can remember all kinds of lawn ornaments (before the plastic pink flamingos), puzzles, tie racks, signs and more.

HISTORY

These projects were proudly made as projects are made today.

It is my thought, that in the late thirties and early forties people made jig saw projects to sell to help supplement their income due to the Depression, just as they did in the 1880s.

By the early fifties, scrolling pretty much died out. Except for school woodshops, the jig saw was forgotten.

In 1974 Helmut Abel of Germany obtained a patent on a constant-tension scroll saw. It was a well-designed and well-made saw. It is interesting to compare the 1880 "New Rogers" saw with the new Hegner saw.

In 1978, Advanced Machinery Imports, Ltd., of New Castle, Delaware, brought the Hegner scroll saw to America. I can remember thinking the first time I saw one of these scroll saws with the skinny blade, "Who in the world would want a dumb-looking machine like this? What in the world can you do with a blade that thin?" —Boy, was I wrong in my thinking!

In those days, no one demonstrated scroll saws at woodworking shows. The saws just sat on the show floor with a piece of pine on the saw table. The saws were plugged in, ready to go, so all those walking by could try cutting a piece of wood. At the time, I really could not see any use for a saw like this. Lucky for all of us, Patrick Spielman did see a use for it and came up with a series of great books touting the scroll saw and what great things a woodworker could really do with it. I consider Pat the "Father" of scroll sawing today.

In 1982 R. B. Industries (R. B. I.) developed a line of constant-tension scroll saws. They were the first scroll saws made in America. The 'R' and the 'B' in the company name are from the company's original owner, R. B. Rice.

In 1986, Tom Sommerville came up with a unique mechanical way to move a scroll saw blade up and down. He developed and introduced a scroll saw under the trade name of Excalibur. This saw is manufactured today in Scarborough, Ontario, Canada.

Since the introduction of the first Hegner in 1978, many other less-expensive scroll saw brands have been introduced to the woodworking industry. Many have come and gone but the better ones still remain today.

As this book is written and published, the latest scroll saw is the new DeWalt (model #DW788). It was introduced in 1997 and has many new features.

At this time, I know of seventeen companies that manufacture and offer hobby scroll saws. They sell from $89 to $1200. (Hegner has a special commercial grade scroll saw that sells for $2,400.) These saws are improving all the time.

Pattern sheet No. 237 (see page 5) from Miller Falls Co. Note prices of thin wood

TYPES OF SAW MECHANISMS

There are four types of scroll saw mechanisms:

1. Rigid Arm
2. Parallel Arm
3. Double Parallel Link Arm
4. "C" Arm
5. Oscillating Loop

Each has its own advantages and, in some cases, disadvantages.

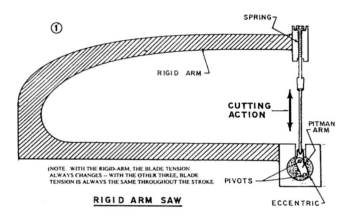

(NOTE: WITH THE RIGID-ARM, THE BLADE TENSION ALWAYS CHANGES -- WITH THE OTHER THREE, BLADE TENSION IS ALWAYS THE SAME THROUGHOUT THE STROKE

RIGID ARM SAW

1. Rigid Arm

An example of the rigid arm saw would be the 1935 Delta jig saw. This saw had a heavy cast iron rigid arm that held the top and bottom of the blade at the ends of the arms. The motor pulled the blade down and a spring brought the blade up. This motion gave a perfect up-and-down blade motion. The blade tension always changed as the blade tightened on the down stroke, but loosen on the up stroke. This gave a very rough saw kerf. Unfortunately, more time is spent sanding the edges of the cut than cutting out the project. This mechanism was very popular from 1935 to 1975. Most saws took the large pin-type saw blades, so could not do complicated fret work projects. This saw was very expensive in its day—in the sixties it sold for around $1700. Today, as far as I know, Powermatic Corporation is the only company offering this type of a saw.

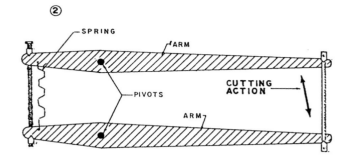

PARALLEL ARM

2. Parallel Arm

The parallel arm mechanism has two arms that pivot about two points (bearings). The two arms move up and down parallel to each other. This mechanism is the very same as it was in the early 1880, pedal-powered scroll saws. The parallel arm mechanism gives an almost perfectly straight up-and-down blade motion. This near-perfect perpendicular motion allows you to make very sharp corners and precision cuts because the wood does not have a tendency to "pick up" on tight turns. If the blade breaks, the top arm stops immediately and swings up out of the way. This is an important safety feature.

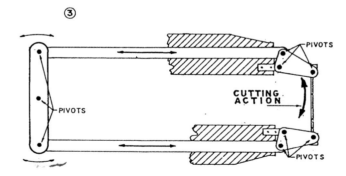

DOUBLE PARALLEL LINK

3. Double Parallel Link Arm

The double parallel link arm scroll saw mechanism incorporated two horizontal rods that move back and forth horizontally. This back and forth motion of the rods are converted to an up and down motion at the ends of the rods. It is the up-and-down motion that creates the "arched" blade motion. This system gives a smooth blade motion with little vibration.

The only drawback I see is if the blade breaks, the top half of the broken blade still moves up and down until the motor is turned off. This could be dangerous.

④

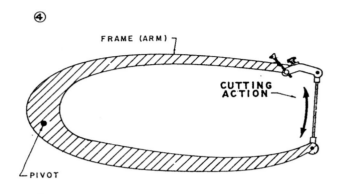

'C' FRAME

4. "C" Arm

The "C" arm scroll saw mechanism uses an arm in the shape of a "C" with the blade attached to the ends of the arm. The "C" arm pivots about a single pivot point. Using this design, the blade moves in an arc — not straight up and down. This gives an aggressive cut but can not make sharp turns without burning the edge of the wood or picking up the wood as you turn. For your information and as a safety point, if the blade breaks, the top half of the broken blade will keep moving until the motor is turned off. This could be a dangerous situation.

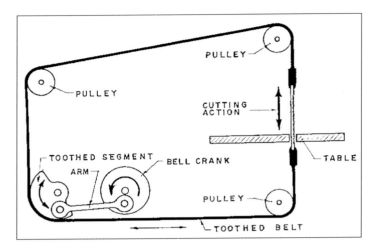

5. Oscillating Loop

This is the newest scroll saw mechanism to enter into the world of scrolling. The oscillating loop mechanism uses a flexible, toothed belt that moves back and forth through a series of pulleys. This motion gives a perfect up-and-down blade motion without any vibration. It is smooth and quiet. The top speed is only 1350 strokes per minute; but because of the long 1 1/2" stroke, it is one of the fastest cutting scroll saws.

Note: The machine will stop immediately if the blade breaks.

TODAY'S SCROLL SAWS

NOTE: Joyce and I do not endorse any brand of scroll saw or any saw accessory. This is an *individual* choice. The only important saw feature to take into consideration is the blade connect/disconnect system.

A quick, tool-less blade changing feature is the only recommendation we do advocate. This is very important and will make your scrolling a lot more fun.

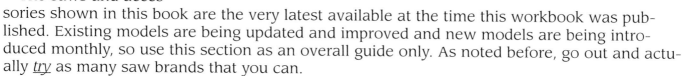

The saws and accessories shown in this book are the very latest available at the time this workbook was published. Existing models are being updated and improved and new models are being introduced monthly, so use this section as an overall guide only. As noted before, go out and actually *try* as many saw brands that you can.

Choose the saw that fits you and your needs. The only recommendation we make is to purchase the *best* saw you can afford in your "price range" so you won't want to trade up later.

► **DELTA**
Telephone: 800-438-2486
Model: # 40-570
Motor: Variable speed scroll saw
Blade size/type: 5" pinless
Throat Depth: 16"
Depth of cut: 2"
Cuts per minute: 600-1650 variable speed
Table Size: 11 ¾" diameter
Table Tilt: 45 degrees left, 0 degrees right
Weight: 60 lbs.
Other features: Parallel arm, quick release blade tension (up front), quick charge blade holder, electronic variable speed.
Note: Delta also makes a top-rated C-arm saw, Model Q3, 40-650. If you wish to consider a C-arm saw, you might consider this model.

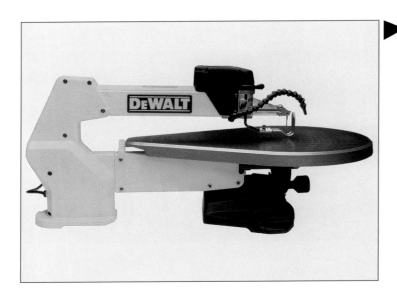

► **DEWALT (Black & Decker)**
Telephone: 800-433-9258
Model: #DW788
Motor: Variable speed
Blade size/type: 5" pinless
Throat depth: 20"
Stroke length: 3/4"
Depth of cut: 2"
Cuts per minute: 400 to 1750
Table size: 16 x 23³/4"
Table tilt: 45 degrees left, 45 degrees right
Weight: 56 lbs.
Other features: Heavy-duty stand (optional), flexible dust blower, double parallel link arm design, fixed-position blade clamps, up-front controls, tool-free blade change system, single-lever tensioning system, upper arm lifts out of the way for threading blades into wood.

DREMEL
Telephone: 800-437-3635
Model: #1672
Motor: 2 speed
Blade size/type: 5" pinned/pinless
Throat depth: 16"
Stroke Length: 3/4"
Cuts per minute: 2 speed 890/1790
Table size: 12" diameter
Table tilt: 45 degrees left, 0 degrees right
Other features: Vacuum hose dust port, quick change blade adaptation, saw dust blower, easy access door to access lower blade assembly

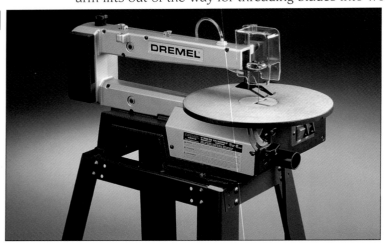

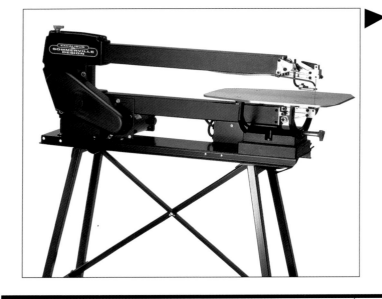

► **EXCALIBUR**
Telephone: 800-357-4118 (Sommerville Design), 800-462-3353 (Seyco), 800-598-2743 (Treeline)
Model: # EX-30
Motor: Variable speed (full torque DC motor)
Blade size/type: 5" pinless
Throat depth: 30"
Stroke Length: .70
Depth of cut: 2"
Cuts per minute: 0 – 1650
Table size: 12" x 17"
Table tilt: 45 degrees left, 30 degrees right
Weight: 65 lbs.
Other features: Quick blade changing system, heavy-duty stand, front quick blade tensioner, unique double parallel link drive system, top arm lifts for easy blade insertion.

▶ **ECLIPSE**
Telephone: 804–779–2478
Model: #2003
Motor: 3 Amps (DC) (SCR)
Blade size/type: 5" pinless
Throat depth: 20"
Stroke Length: $1^1/2$"
Depth of cut: $1^1/2$"
Cuts per minute: Variable speed 200–1350
Table size: 15" x 23"
Weight: 90 lbs. (C.I. Tade)
Other features: Hour meter, built-in Halogen light, automatic stop, will not start if tension is not tight.

HEGNER
Telephone: 800-727-6553
Model: #M18V (Multimax)
Motor: 2.83 Amps
Blade size/type: 5" pinless
Throat depth: 18"
Stroke Length: $3/4$"
Depth of cut: 2 5/8"
Cuts per minute: Variable speed 400 – 1700 RPM
Table size: 9" x 17"
Table Tilt: 45 degrees left, 12 degrees right
Weight: 56 lbs.
Other features: Slotted work table, front quick lock tension release system, saw dust blower, induction motor.

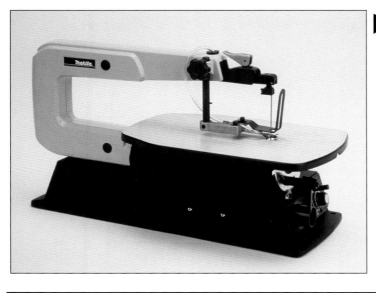

▶ **MAKITA**
Telephone: 800-462-5482
Model: #SJ401
Motor: 1.2 Amps/variable speed
Blade size/type: 5" plain/pin end
Throat depth: 16"
Stroke length: $7/8$"
Depth of cut: 2"
Cuts per minute: 400 – 1600 variable speed
Table size: $9^3/8$" x $14^3/4$"
Table tilt: 45 degrees left, 15 degrees right
Weight: 31.4 lbs.
Other features: Built-in dust blower, tool-free blade clamp, up-front blade tensioning level, vacuum port for efficient dust collecting, parallel arm.

SCROLL SAWS

P.S. WOOD

Telephone: 800-939-4414
Model: #21
Motor: 2.2 Amps
Blade size/type: 5" pinless blade
Throat depth: 21"
Stroke Length: 1"
Depth of cut: $2^3/4$"
Cuts per minute: 5 speed: 170/450/790/1140/1370
Table size: 14" x 22 $^3/4$"
Table Tilt: 45 degrees left, 35 degrees right
Weight: 90 lbs.
Other features: Quick blade change, constant tension, parallel arm, double arm stanchions (eliminates side-to-side blade movement), 5-year warrantee, 30-day money back guarantee.

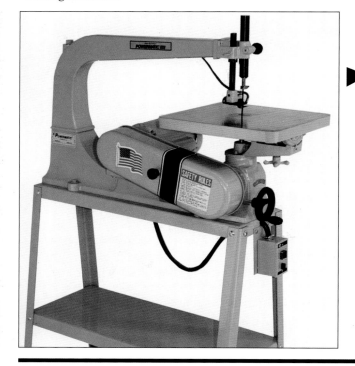

PRO-TECH POWER

Telephone: 800-888-6603
Model: #3303
Motor: 1.2 Amps / variable speed
Blade size/type: 5" pinned/pinless
Throat depth: 16"
Stroke Length: $^7/8$"
Depth of cut: 2"
Cuts per minute: 400 – 1600 (variable speed)
Table size: $9^3/8$" x $14^3/4$"
Table tilt: 45 degrees left, 0 degrees right
Weight: 34 lbs.
Other features: Direct drive motor, 30-day customer satisfaction guarantee, toll free technical assistance, sawdust blower, vacuum port, storage area out of the way, quick and easy blade transfer and easy control of blade tension.

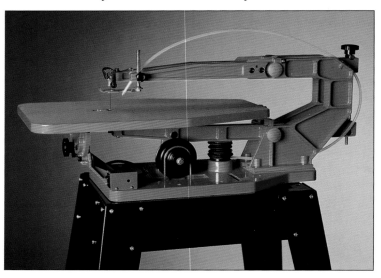

POWERMATIC

Telephone: 800-248-0144
Model: #95-24
Motor: $^1/3$ H.P. (4 speed)
Blade size/type: 5" plain end
Throat depth: 24"
Depth of cut: $1^3/4$"
Cuts per minute: 807 – 1653 variable speed
Table size: 14" x 15"
Table tilt: 15 degrees left, 45 degrees right
Weight: 200 lbs.
Other features: Heavy-duty stand, blade guide for precise blade alignment, built-in blower, perfect up/down blade motion

RIGID

Telephone: 800-325-1184
Model: #SS1650
Motor: 2 Amp
Blade size/type: 5" long pinless
Throat depth: 16"
Stroke Length: $7/8$"
Depth of cut: 2"
Cuts per minute: 500-1700 variable speed
Table tilt: 5 degrees left, 47 degrees right
Weight: 35 lbs.
Other features: Tool-less blade changer, built-in saw dust blower, on-board blade storage, simple "push-on" and "push-off" switch, new from the popular Emerson Tool Co.

▶ **R.B.I.**
Telephone: 800-487-2623
Model: #226
Motor: Variable speed
Blade size/type: 5" pinless
Throat depth: 26"
Stroke length: $7/8$"
Depth of cut: $2^5/8$"
Cuts per minute: 300 – 1725 (variable speed)
Table size: $14^3/4$" dia.
Table tilt: 45 degrees left, 45 degrees right
Weight: 97 lbs.
Other features: Special DC motor with trust ball, heavy-duty steel legs (included), front cam – over tension and upper blade holder (quick change), safety stop and spring (stops arm if blade breaks), exclusive rear cam for blade tensioning, new adjustable dust blower from side.

▶ **RYOBI**
Telephone: 800-525-2579
Model: #SC155
Motor: 1.6 Amp – variable speed
Blade size/type: 5" pinned / pinless
Throat depth: 16"
Depth of cut: 2"
Cuts per minute: 500 – 1700 variable speed
Table tilt: 15 degrees left, 45 degrees right
Other features: Tool-less blade changing system, dual knob, cam-activated blade tensioning system, positive 0-degree stop, blade storage, low vibration, made by Emerson Tool Co.

SHOPSMITH

Telephone: 800-543-7586

Model: #555685

Motor: 1.7 Amps

Blade size/type: 5" pinless

Throat depth: 20"

Stroke length: $7/8$"

Depth of cut: 2"

Cuts per minute: 500–1450

Table size: 16" x $23^7/8$"

Table tilt: 45 degrees left and right

Weight: 85 lbs.

Other features: Quick release tensioning and tool-less blade removal, variable speed ($1/8$ HP), parallel arm system, blower system.

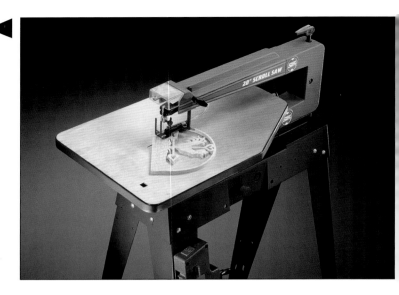

TRADESMAN

Telephone: 800-243-5114

Model: #8368

Motor: 1.7 Amp ball bearing

Blade size/type: 5" pinned/pinless

Throat depth: 16"

Stroke length: $7/8$"

Depth of cut: 2" maximum

Cuts per minute: 400 – 1800 variable speed

Table size: $12^3/4$" x 16"

Table tilt: 0 degrees, 45 degrees right-left

Weight: 45 lbs.

Other features: Speed-lock blade change system (no blade holders required), built-in blower system (from side), up-front speed control, adjustable light, built-in storage case, parallel arm.

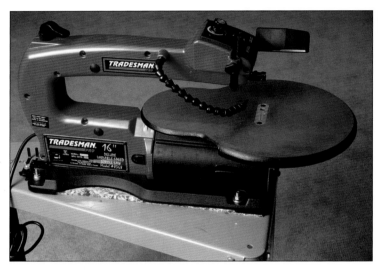

PROXXON

Telephone: 866–776–9832

Model: DSH

Motor: 2 speed

Blade size/type: 5" pinless and pin blades

Throat depth: 15 $3/4$"

Stroke length: $3/4$"

Depth of cut: 2"

Cuts per minute: 900–1500

Table size: 14.25" x 7.1"

Table tilt: 45 degrees

Weight: 44 lbs.

Other features: Cast iron base, air blower, ball bearing direct drive, uses pin or pinless blades, uses T-Allen key.

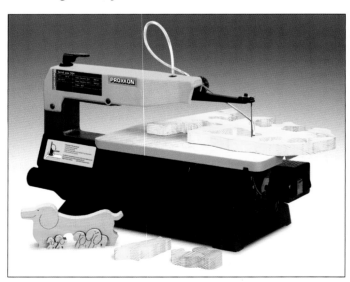

SCROLL SAW BLADES

A complete book could be written on scroll saw blades alone. There are many kinds and sizes of blades—the beginning scroller could very easily get very confused in choosing the right blade for the right job.

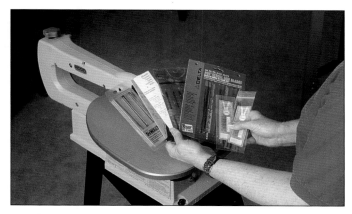

There are two major kinds of blades, plain-end or pin-end types. It is highly recommended that you do not use the pin-end type saw or blades. Thus, pin saw blades will not be covered in this workbook.

Plain-end blades are five inches long and will fit most scroll saws. (Note: I find I have to trim off $1/8$ inch from the standard five-inch-length blade when using the sixteen-inch Delta scroll saw.)

IMPORTANT: Remember the teeth must always point down. Be sure to check this when installing the blade.

Very briefly the major seven types of blades are:

1. Standard tooth blades
2. Skip-tooth blades
3. Double-tooth blades
4. Reverse-tooth blades
5. Precision-ground blades
6. Spiral-tooth blades
7. Crown-tooth blades

1. Standard Tooth Blades

The teeth are all the same size and distance apart on standard tooth blades. There are two major kinds: wood blades and metal blades. The wood blades have larger teeth and more space between the teeth. They are designed to clear the sawdust as you cut. The metal blades have much smaller teeth and less space between teeth. I find these a bit noisy.

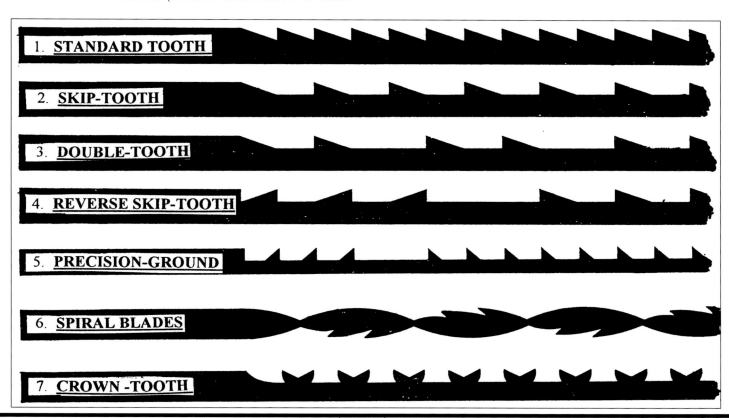

1. **STANDARD TOOTH**

2. **SKIP-TOOTH**

3. **DOUBLE-TOOTH**

4. **REVERSE SKIP-TOOTH**

5. **PRECISION-GROUND**

6. **SPIRAL BLADES**

7. **CROWN -TOOTH**

BLADES

2. Skip-tooth Blades

These blades are similar to the standard tooth blades, but every other tooth is missing. The space (gullet) between teeth is much wider and keeps the blade cooler. Personally, I like these for most work. They are especially good for beginning scrollers.

3. Double-tooth Blades

This blade is a skip-tooth blade with a large space between sets of two teeth. These blades cut slightly slower but leave a very smooth cut.

4. Reverse Skip-tooth Blades

This blade is exactly like the regular skip-tooth blade, except the last few bottom teeth point upward. This is great for preventing tear-out or splintering on the bottom of the cut and for use with plywood.

When using a reverse skip-tooth blade you must set the blade in the clamps so that only two or three teeth are pointing up above the table top when the saw arm is in its highest position. You may have to trim a little from the bottom of the blade to accomplish this.

5. Precision-ground Blades

These blades are actually a skip-tooth blade with small teeth that have been ground to shape rather than simply filed. These blades are much sharper, cut in a straight line and leave a very smooth surface. Personally, I find they are great blades but very aggressive and unforgiving. I do not recommend them for the beginner.

6. Spiral Blades

These blades are simply a group of blades twisted together so there are teeth all the way around. You can cut in all directions without turning the wood. There are a few applications for this kind of blade, but they leave a very rough, wide surface, cannot make a tight or sharp corner and have a tendency to stretch as you use them. I do not recommend these blades except for special applications.

3. Crown-tooth Blades

This is a totally new design in scroll saw blades. The teeth are shaped like a crown with a space between each crown. The nice part is that the blade can be put in either way, so there is no upsidedown with these blades. I find they cut a little slower than a regular blade, but they are good for cutting plastic or Plexiglas®.

When the blade dulls you can reverse ends and have a sharp blade again.

Other Special Blades

There are special blades designed to cut metal, plastic and even glass. Check them out as you advance in your scrolling. You may want to use them for special applications. Most all saw companies provide special blades.

At the time of developing this workbook, Olson Saw Company came out with a new PGT double-tooth scroll saw blade in sizes 5, 7 and 9. This new ground-tooth blade has superior performance and produces a super-smooth finish.

For Beginning Scrollers

To eliminate all confusion about blades and for all projects in this book, only standard skip-tooth blades will be recommended. Purchase a few dozen each of #3 and #5 skip-tooth blades and a dozen crown-tooth blades.

As you master the scroll saw, experiment with other types of blades. Find the one or ones that "fit" you and with which you are most comfortable. Don't go out and purchase a dozen of each kind available; you won't use them.

Choosing the Correct Blade

Consider the following criteria when choosing blades:
- Material thickness—Thicker materials require bigger blades.
- Material hardness—Harder substances require larger teeth and/or a different type of blade.
- Complexity—A very complex pattern will require a blade with small teeth.

Always use the largest size blade you can and still get the desired results you want.

Tension of the Blade

Each saw brand has a particular way to apply tension to the blades. A few steps are the same regardless of the brand or method. Make sure the blade is straight inside the clamps and the teeth are pointing down. With very fine teeth, such as those on a #0/2 blade, it is hard to see the direction of the teeth. Simply, run your index finger lightly up and down along the front of the blade (with motor off). You will feel a somewhat smooth feel when going in the direction the teeth are facing and a very rough feeling when going the opposite direction the teeth are facing. Thus, if the teeth are facing down, as they should, you will have a rough feeling as you slide your finger up and a smooth feeling as you slide your finger down. (Remember do not over tighten the blade in the end supports.)

Once the blade is in correctly, apply tension to it. The tensioning adjustment is either in front or in back of your saw. See your owner's manual for directions for your particular saw.

Many beginners have a tendency to apply too much tension. Apply only enough tension to hold the blade somewhat rigid as it cuts. (You can allow a little flex, but not too much.)

I pluck the blade like a banjo string. When the blade has little or no tension, it will have a dull "plunking" sound. As you apply tension the dull "plunking" will turn into a clear musical note

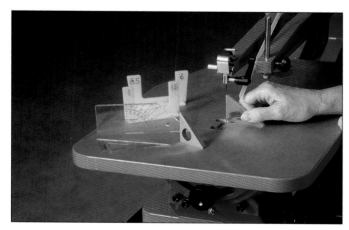

sound (ping). I tune to "C", but you will have to experiment to see what works for you.

Another way to apply the correct tension is to tighten the blade so it flexes. (No more than 1/8"

sideways.) After a while you will know where the correct tension is. If your blade wanders or bows, your tension is too loose; if it breaks frequently, it is too tight.

SQUARING UP THE BLADE

The blade must be exactly 90 degrees to the table. It is very important that you check almost daily, especially if you occasionally cut on an angle.

You can purchase a beautiful brass triangle, an inexpensive plastic triangle or a set of Accu-angles to check the 90 degree angle. These are nice, but I find an inexpensive and easy way is to simply use a 1 3/4"-thick piece of scrap wood.

Simply make a shallow cut into the wood about 1/16" deep, then turn the wood around to the back of the blade (do not turn it upside-down) and slide the back of the blade back into the cut. If it slides in nicely, the table is square or at 90 degrees. Adjust, if necessary, until it does slide into the saw kerf. Make sure you double check this every time you use the saw.

ACCESSORIES FOR THE SCROLL SAW

To get the most out of your scroll saw and enjoy it even more, you might want to consider some of the accessories available.

Stand

If you add a stand, you free up your bench space. A stand gives you a chance to work all around your scroll saw. With the scroll saw on a bench you tend to have more vibration; the stand helps to eliminate most of this vibration.

Personally, I prefer a heavy welded stand as it will help absorb any vibration. Stands come with three or four legs.

Some saws have built-in stands like the P.S. Wood saws.

I like the three legged stands, as they are self leveling. Note that your stand and saw should be placed on a solid surface. If your shop is on a wooden floor, your saw might tend to be noisy and vibrate. A cement floor provides a great solid surface and will help eliminate any vibration.

The October 1996 issue of *WOOD Magazine* features a stand that you can make yourself. Check your local library for a back issue.

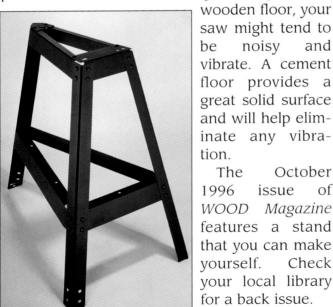

Stool

Some scrollers like to sit while they cut. If you are one of those scrollers, choose a comfortable stool at an appropriate height. You might want to add a pillow for comfort. Try to find a three-legged stool so you won't have any rocking.

TRADESMAN

Lights

Lighting is very important. You do not want any shadows on the pattern or blade as you are cutting. Some saws come with a light that attaches to the stand or saw, itself. A magnifying light is also available. Some people use the magnifier to enlarge the pattern while they cut. (For very small projects some people find this helpful; others find it annoying.)

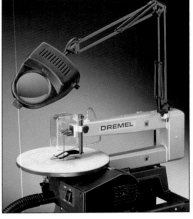

DREMEL

Foot Switch

The foot switch frees up both of your hands. It makes the scroll saw even safer to use as you can start or stop the blade and still hold the wood in place at the same time. The foot switch will actually save you time on complicated projects with many interior cuts because you do not have to reach for the switch for each interior cut.

The foot switch simplifies and speeds up the entire process. There are two major kinds of foot switches: air-operated and electronic types. Both work equally well.

Note: I feel a foot switch is not really needed if you have a DeWalt scroll saw or Excalibur saw. The on-off switch is up front and easily accessible for quick use.

Variable Speed

Cutting speed is measured in strokes per minute. Most one-speed saws cut from 1200 to 1800 strokes per minute. This speed is fine for most wood. Variable speed cuts from 400 to 1800 strokes per minute. This is important if you cut thin veneers, plastic, brass, steel or even glass (with special blades). Another choice would be a two-speed scroll saw. Personally, I find that in a two-speed saw, slow speed is too slow and high speed is too fast.

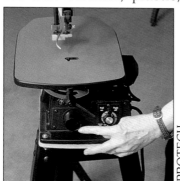

Quick-release Blade Clamp

Blade changing is one of the most important features of a scroll saw. If your saw uses a key or special wrench to change the blade, look for a good, quick-release blade clamp kit that will fit your saw. If you can't get an efficient quick-release clamp, sell the saw — you will be nothing but frustrated with scrolling!

Blower

At this time I believe all scroll saws have a blower. Some have an adjustable blower tube that blows the dust to the side or away from you. Some still have blowers that blow the dust toward the scroller. I know some scrollers who place a fan at the left side of the saw and blow the dust to the right, away from them.

Vacuum

Some saw companies provide a vacuum port.

Although it could be noisy, a vacuum is an excellent way to keep the dust down. There are quiet vacuums available today.

Floor Mat

If you are going to stand in one location for an extended length of time, a floor mat is something you should consider using. They are rather inexpensive and will add a lot of comfort.

Saw Covers

There are commercially made saw covers available.

If your particular saw brand does not have a cover available you can use a large trash bag as a scroll saw cover to keep out any dust.

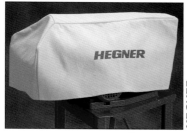

Use another trash bag, attached by masking tape to the front of the saw, to collect small pieces of wood and dust. A trash bag taped to the front of the saw will really speed up your clean-up efforts.

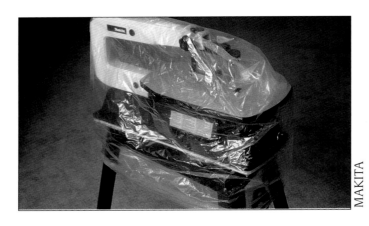

MAKITA

PS WOOD

Scroll Saw "Handy Top"

The "handy top" is 16" x 24" in size and can be added to any scroll saw. It provides a friction-free work surface and creates a high-contrast, non-glare background.

Related Tools

A wonderful power tool that really speeds up scroll sawing is a thickness sander. A thickness

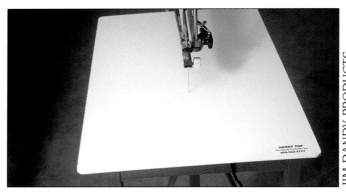

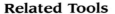

JIM DANDY PRODUCTS

sander such as the 16-32 Plus Performax can sand small finished scroll saw pieces.

You can sand your wood to an exact thickness. If your project calls for 3/16"-thick wood, you can purchase 5/16" to 1/4" thick and easily sand it down to the 3/16" thickness. If you have a piece that has to be 3/16" thick, you can cut it out of 1/4" thick material and after cutting out,

sand the pieces down to 3/16" thick, which removes all rough edges. Pieces come out perfect every time. RBI also features a thickness sander.

PERFORMAX PRODUCTS

EXCALIBER

PAUL REVERE

Arm Lift (DeWalt and Excalibur saws only)

A great accessory to add to your DeWalt or Excalibur saw is an arm lift. There are two kinds of arm lifts: spring-operated and foot-operated.

Shaper/Router Table With Rotary Tool

A very handy tool to be used with scroll saws is a small shaper/router. This tool will allow you to very easily and quickly round or chamfer edges. This creates a wonderful "finished" effect. These shapers/router tables are an inexpensive tool and a great tool to use in conjunction with the scroll saw.

DREMEL

FEATURES TO LOOK FOR IN A SCROLL SAW

Price

For most of us price is the limiting factor. Today hobby scroll saws sell from $89 to $1200.

When you establish an affordable price range for you, shop around and actually try each saw. Go to woodworking shows, where you can try all the different brands. Do not buy a saw out of a box without trying it. All saws have their good and bad points, so take your time and find the one that fits your budget and your needs.

For years, we have conducted scroll saw classes. In our classes we have one or two models of most all major brands. Throughout the 16 hours of classes, the students rotate around the various saws and get to use them all. By the end of the two days, most students settle on one or two models that they really like. The saw has to "fit" you! Each brand has some extra unique feature or features that the others do not have. These various features are either very important or less important to each person. Again, try before buying!

We have had students tell us they "wouldn't own a red saw..." "Couldn't stand a saw with three legs..." "Would only buy an American-made tool..." Some students loved a particular blade changing system and simply hated another. There are so many variables you must try each saw that fits into your price range.

Use

If you are going to use your saw on the occasional weekends as a hobby, perhaps spending $180 will do.

If you're going to go into business making projects to sell, you should consider a saw in the $1200 price range. (For high quantity production you might have to spend as much as $2400.)

Remember, regardless if you are a hobbyist or a professional scroller, **you should purchase the absolute best saw you can afford!** You will have better and quicker blade changing ability, you will have a smoother vibration-free

saw, a quiet saw, and you will enjoy the saw so much more than if you had scrimped and bought an inexpensive saw. ***Buy a saw you want and can enjoy using.***

Thickness of the Cut

Saws make a 2"-thick minimum to 2⅝" maximum cut. Most saw cuts you will make are ¾"-inch thick. If you stack cut, you will probably cut up to 1¾" maximum thickness.

DELTA

Throat Length

Throat length is the distance between the saw blade and the back of the saw. Sixteen inches is minimum and thirty inches is maximum. For years, I have found the eighteen-inch throat length adequate for anything I have ever wanted to do.

RYOBI

Safety

Does the upper arm or top half of the scroll saw blade stop if the blade brakes? This is an important safety feature to consider. Keep in mind, only parallel arm saws can offer this safety feature. Blades don't break very often, but they do break!

Table Top Tilt

Many scroll saws tilt only one way. Usually to the left, forty-five degrees. Others tilt both ways. The more expensive saws tilt 45 degrees each way. (This is something you should consider.)

Dust Blowers

Most all scroll saws today have dust blowers. A few saw blowers can be adjusted to blow the dust away to the side which is an excellent feature.

Weight

If you plan on moving your scroll saw a lot, weight could be a factor. Scroll saw weights vary from about thirty pounds to one hundred pounds. (Powermatic's #95 weights two hundred twenty pounds. This is actually a fixed arm saw and wouldn't be moved much.)

Warranty

Scroll saw warranties vary from one year to six years. I have found most scroll saws we have used in our scroll saw classes have been very dependable. We have had very few problems, but there have been a few. You should inquire what you have to do in the event of a problem. Some companies have you wrap the saw up and send it back. This is a nuisance and a bit costly.

Blade Tension

The scroll saw blade should be adjustable. Some blade tensions adjust from the front and others from the back.

This is something you should consider if you

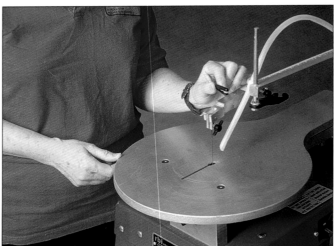

do a lot of blade changing. The front adjustment is easier.

Pin-end Versus Plain-end Blades

If you really want to do scrolling and enjoy it, do not purchase a pin-end scroll saw. Consider a plain-end blade saw only. The pin-end saws require a large diameter starter hole and blades are usually very large in size.

Other Features of Note

Hegner features a slot that makes inserting the blade in place very simple and quick.

DeWalt has an on-off switch up front. A

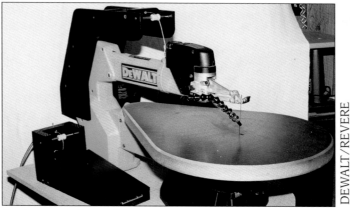

Foot-operated arm lift.

DEWALT/REVERE

Storage drawer for blades.

MAKITA

handy feature.

Rigid and a few other brand models have a handy up-front, blade storage area.

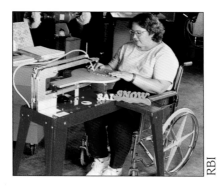

RBI

Wheel Chair Accessible

A few scroll saw manufacturers have special scroll saws and stands that have various features for the handicapped. Scrolling is an excellent hobby for the physically challenged.

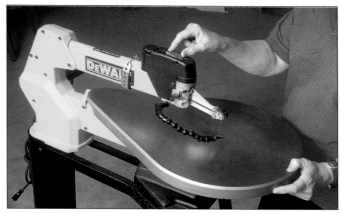

Switch located up front.

DEWALT

HEGNER

Scrolling With Children

Today, woodworking is not offered in schools. In my day we all were required to take "Manual Arts" or "Wood Shop."

Children today, as a rule, do not have this opportunity. The scroll saw is a great tool to teach children eye and hand coordination and a wonderful way to introduce them to the world of woodworking. Try to pass on your love for woodworking to your children and grandchildren.

Blade Changing

I purposely left the blade changing feature for last. We feel **blade changing is the most important feature of the scroll saw!** Nothing will take away from the fun and relaxation the scroll saw provides more than having a saw with a difficult way of changing the blade.

If you do any, or plan to do any interior cuts at all, you will want a saw with a tool-less quick blade disconnect. When you are looking and trying scroll saws, have a salesperson show you how the blade is changed. Then try changing the blade yourself. (The salesperson has probably practiced blade changing thousands of times and can make it look very easy.) The blade changing ability should be easy for you. Today's scroll saws vary a lot, so find one with which you are comfortable and that you will enjoy.

After you have purchased a saw, what to cut and what to cut it out of come next. Let's take a look at patterns first, then move on to the different materials you can use on a scroll saw.

SCROLL SAW PATTERNS

Excellent patterns of all kinds and levels can be purchased.

The least expensive way to get a library of scroll saw patterns is to buy various books of scroll saw patterns. Even if you like only half of the patterns in a particular book, the price per pattern is still lower than purchasing individual patterns.

After choosing a pattern that you'd like to try, copy the pattern. You can have copies made at any library or at any business establishment that makes copies for the public. Some scrollers prefer having copies made in red so they can see the lines of the pattern better against the black blade. Do not use the actual page from the book or the actual patterns; you will destroy the book and limit the pattern to one-time use. You may want to make the same project again.

Consider enlarging or reducing the original pattern to fit a particular space or application. A three-inch diameter window hanger pattern could be enlarged to seven or eight inches in diameter and used as a trivet. A wall shelf might have to be reduced to fit the space between windows.
Note: If you enlarge or reduce a pattern you should enlarge or reduce the material thickness, so that the material thickness is still in proportion to the pattern design.

Keep in mind, any pattern can be modified or changed with a copy machine. It will than be your own creation!

Attaching the Paper Pattern to the Wood

There are various methods to attach the pattern to the wood. You can use rubber cement, glue sticks or adhesive spray, any of which can be purchased at office supply stores. I have used them all, but I prefer adhesive spray. If you use adhesive spray, purchase temporary or re-positional adhesive spray.

I make a "spray booth" by folding back the top flaps of a cardboard box that is about 2' x 2' x

1¹/₂'. Put the box on its side. Place the pattern in the box, face down, and lightly spray the back of the pattern. You will have to experiment a few times until you have it just right. Allow a minute or two for the adhesive to set, then apply it to the wood. Be sure the wood is dust free and take care to note the direction of the grain.

To Remove the Pattern after Cutting

After the pattern is completely cut out, remove the pattern. Put paint thinner (turpentine or mineral spirits) in a spray bottle. Simply apply a light spray coat over the paper pattern, let it sit for twenty or thirty seconds. The pattern should slide right off. Let the wood dry before lightly sanding it.

SELECTING MATERIAL

There are many places to obtain wood. It is usually less expensive (and you can pick it over) if you have a local wood supplier. If not, there are some wonderful specialty wood companies that can supply most anything you need. (See the Appendix at the back of this book.)

To get started, use a softwood such as pine, spruce, aspen or basswood. These woods are easy to cut and are good woods for beginners. They are also a good choice if you plan to paint your project. Be sure the wood you choose is knot-free.

When you become more comfortable with scrolling, use hardwoods such as maple, walnut, or oak. Maple, birch or cherry are a hardwood and are an excellent choice of wood to use for complicated, intricate projects.

Open-grained wood such as oak, ash,

mahogany or walnut have a tendency to split. Keep this in mind and take care when cutting these woods.

Note: Hardwood finishes beautifully. In fact, if I use a very nice piece of wood with a lot of character, I simply put a coat or two of clear satin tung oil on it and let it "mellow" with time. Always try to find and use wood with a nice grain pattern and a lot of "character."

It is always nice (and less expensive) to use a local wood, if possible. I personally love cherry, and it is a beautiful wood, but I find it hard to cut and it has a tendency to burn in tight turns. If you do use cherry you should slow your saw down slightly and cut slower than normal. A tip for cutting cherry: Put a layer of clear wrapping (shipping) tape on top of the pattern. The tape will lubricate the blade to help eliminate the burning.

Plywood has a place, but most plywood has no "character" and does not finish well. Inexpensive plywood does make great backing boards or can be put to use on other pieces that can't be seen. Unless you are going to paint your project, plywood may not be a good choice.

A high-grade plywood that is faced (both sides) with a nice hard wood such as walnut, cherry, oak or hickory is acceptable, as it has "character," looks like real wood and finishes nicely. For special projects like book markers, which are $1/32$" or $1/64$" thick, micro-thin plywood is the only thing to use.

Regardless of how expensive the wood is, it is your time (labor) that is the largest expense factor. Your finished project will be seen and felt for years to come. The difference between an inexpensive piece of wood or an expensive piece of wood may be as much as double the cost. Regardless of the cost, all your cutting time will still be the same.

For example, you can make a very large, complicated scroll saw clock such as the Chimes of Normandy out of plywood or some other inexpensive wood, and it will cost you $30 or so. You could make the exact same clock out of beautiful birdseye maple for $70. Cutting out the clock will take you the same amount of time whether you use plywood or maple. Figuring that it takes 110 hours to cut out the clock and that your time is

Chimes of Normandy

worth about $10 an hour, the "cost" of cutting and assembly is $1,100. With that in mind, the $40 difference between the cost of the plywood and the cost of the maple becomes insignificant, and the extra value in using the birdseye maple is immeasurable.

Other Materials for Scrolling

You do not have to use only wood to make scroll saw projects. Given the right blade and the correct speed, your saw will cut all kinds of materials. Try using particle board, plastic, Plexiglas, steel, brass and even stone (alabaster is an excellent material to use). Although, I have never cut glass, it can be cut using a diamond-tipped blade. After you master the basics in this workbook, try other materials. You are limited only by your lack of imagination.

Gluing

For most projects a good white glue that dries clear is a good choice. For larger, very complicated projects use an instant glue such as "Hot Stuff" Super 'T'. Super 'T' is also good to glue plastic on other material, other than wood. This glue sets up in about 30 seconds and fills gaps.

GETTING STARTED
Four major steps for all exercises

These four steps will be used at the start of each and every exercise throughout the book. Refer back to them at the start of each exercise and every time you use the scroll saw.

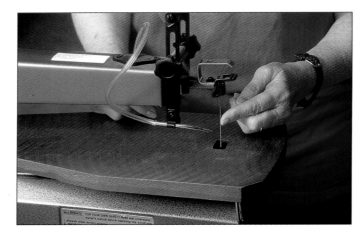

1. Attach the blade to the saw. Make sure the teeth are facing to the front and facing down. You can check this by lightly running your finger up and down on the blade (with the saw off). If correct, your finger will drag on the way up.

2. Check that the blade is at a right angle (90 degrees) to the table top. Use a triangle or the "block of wood" trick (on page 15).

3. Adjust the tension of the blade ("C" pitch or $1/8$" side motion, maximum).

4. Put on safety glasses.

Note before cutting: Most scroll saw blades are somewhat sharper on one side than the other side. The scroll saw blade does not nor will it, cut in an absolute straight line parallel to the edge of the table top. If you have used a band saw, or table saw, the cut is usually parallel and straight to the saw fence or edge of table. With the scroll saw, the blade has a tendency to cut more aggressively on one side than the other side. To cut a straight line with a scroll saw you must feed the pattern into the blade on a slight angle one way or the other and "steer" the wood along the cutting line, similar to driving a car on a road. Don't push the board into the blade — let the blade itself cut through the wood.

Note: Precision ground blades are made much better and tend to follow a straight line better than a regular blade. They are however, much more aggressive thus not recommended for the beginner at this time. Don't forget — Do not push the wood into the blade; let the blade do the cutting.

As with any tool, safety is an important consideration. We have the scroll saw to be a relatively safe tool to operate, but there are still certain safety considerations that should be kept in mind. Most of them are common sense.

- Keep your hands away from the blade. When cutting very small pieces of wood, use a cardboard backing to help you control the wood and ensure that your fingers are away from the blade.

- Use eye gear. It is tempting to opt not to use eye gear when you are working with a scroll saw. Be safe and err on the side of caution.

- Dust masks are optional. The scroll saw makes very little dust, but a mask or a dust blower will help keep what little dust it does make out of your lungs.

- Face masks are also optional. They should, however, be worn when you are working with glass or metal.

- Don't over-do it. If you feel yourself getting tired, take a break. Most accidents in the shop happen when a woodworker is tired and his or her attention is focused elsewhere.

<u>**Objective:**</u> **Practice following straight lines, wavy lines, making sharp corners and turning in place.**

<u>**Materials needed:**</u> (1) $^3/_4$" x 6" - 8" long piece of wood
#5 skip tooth blade

Step   1 Make a copy of Practice Exercise 1 and attach it to a knot-free piece of pine or similar wood.

Step   2 Review the four "Getting Started" steps on page 24.

Step   3 Stand or sit directly _in front of_ the saw. Relax and take a deep breath.

Step   4 Hold your fingers as if you were working on a computer keyboard—use the _tips_ of your fingers. If you are right-handed, use your left hand to lightly hold down the wood. Place your left index finger about 1" directly to the left of the blade. This index finger will help you rotate the wood when you make turns. Use your right hand to _steer_ the wood along the straight line. (If you are left-handed, reverse the instructions.) Remember: Use your finger tips, not your hands and body, to hold and _steer_ the wood, as if you were driving a car along a road.

Step   5 <u>To make a straight cut</u> : Align the blade with the end of the pattern and wood at "A." Take a deep breath and _relax_. Lightly push the wood into the blade; let the blade do the cutting. Again, relax. I cannot stress this enough! Be sure your left hand is _lightly_ holding the wood down. Keep in mind, the teeth of the scroll saw blade are in _front_ of the blade facing you. This is where the blade cuts, not on the side or back of the blade. Many people do not realize this their first time using a scroll saw. Complete the straight line cut. If you get off the line, _slowly_ turn the wood to get back on the line. Do not push the blade sideways. Try one more straight line at "A."

Step   6 <u>To make a curved, wavy line</u>: Follow the same steps as in Step #5. Practice cutting wavy lines along the three lines marked "B."

Step   7 <u>To make sharp turns</u>: Start cutting in at "C." When you reach each large dot on the pattern, stop pushing the wood—_relax_—and back off slightly. With your left index finger

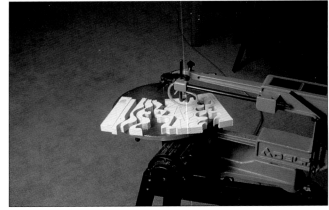

about 1" to the left of the blade, _rotate_ the wood to line up with the direction of the line. Continue cutting. Each time you get to a dot follow the instructions above. (Note: On actual patterns there will <u>not</u> be a dot at any sharp turn. Imagine there is a dot and make turns just as you practiced.)

Step 8 <u>To make turns in place:</u> - Cut in at "D." With your left index finger 1 inch to the left of the blade, rotate the wood at the dot and cut your way back out along the existing saw kerf you just made. Do not back out. Practice at the other "D" lines.

Step 9 Practice making waves, curves and sharp turns at "E." Again, stop at each dot, relax, back off slightly, turn, and cut.

Step 10 If you still have problems and need more practice, make another copy of Practice Exercise 1 and repeat steps 2 through 9.

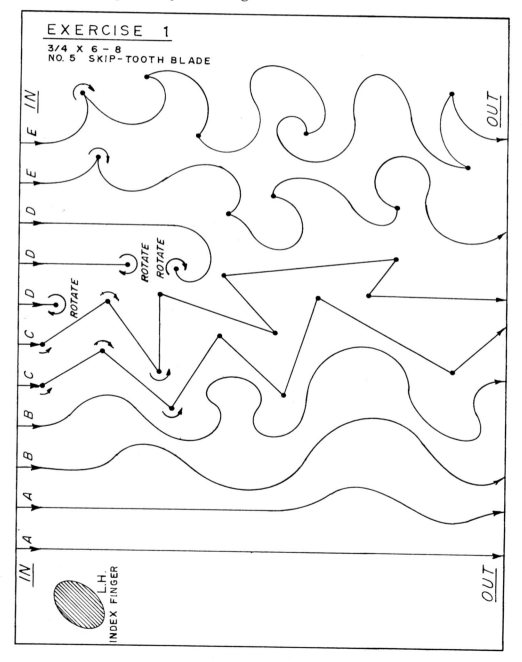

Objective: **To cut out a simple object, following lines to produce a smooth, continuous, flowing cut.**

Materials needed:
(1) 3/4 " x 4¹/₂" - 5¹/₂" long piece of wood
#5 skip tooth blade

Step 1 Make a copy of Practice Exercise 2 and attach it to a knot-free piece of pine or similar wood.

Step 2 Review the four "Getting Started" steps on page 24.

Step 3 Stand or sit directly *in front of* the saw. Relax and take a deep breath.

Step 4 Using only your fingertips and a light touch, cut in as indicated. Make a smooth, continuous, flowing cut all the way around without stopping.

Note: If you wander off the cutting line *outside* of the pattern, stop and back up to where you wandered off. Continue cutting out your pattern (see figure 1). If you wander off the cutting line *inside* of the pattern, keep cutting slowly and smoothly back to the pattern line (see figure 2). Remember, after you remove the pattern from the wood, no one will know you were off the line.

Step 5 When you have the project all cut out, check the edges. You should have a continuous, smooth surface all around. If not, make another copy of the pattern and repeat Step 1 through Step 4 with a new piece of wood until it is perfect.

PRACTICE MAKES PERFECT!

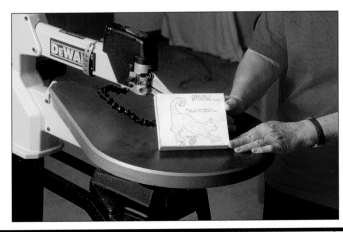

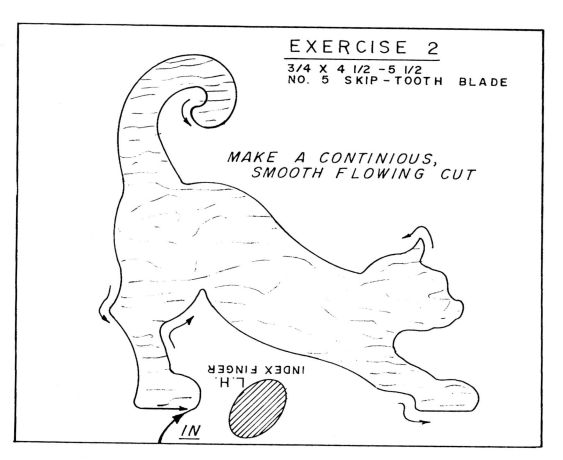

EXERCISE 2
3/4 X 4 1/2 - 5 1/2
NO. 5 SKIP-TOOTH BLADE

MAKE A CONTINIOUS, SMOOTH FLOWING CUT

L.H.
INDEX FINGER

IN

PATTERN

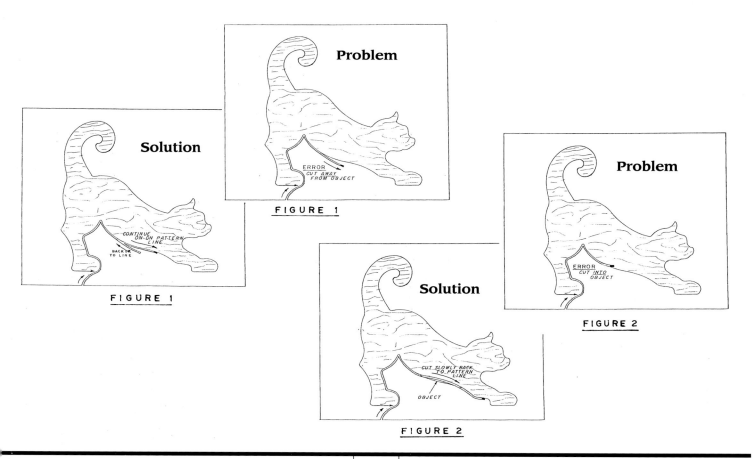

Problem

ERROR
CUT AWAY
FROM OBJECT

FIGURE 1

Solution

CONTINUE
ON-ON PATTERN
LINE

BACK UP
TO LINE

FIGURE 1

Problem

ERROR
CUT INTO
OBJECT

FIGURE 2

Solution

CUT SLOWLY BACK
TO PATTERN
LINE

OBJECT

FIGURE 2

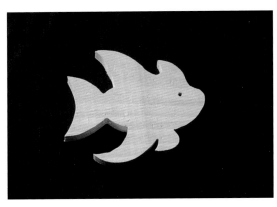

Objective: **To cut out a simple object, following lines to produce a smooth, continuous, flowing cut all around and to produce <u>sharp</u> exterior features using the LOOP METHOD.**

<u>Materials needed:</u>
(1) ³/₄" x 4¹/₂" - 5¹/₂" long piece of wood
#5 skip tooth blade

<u>Step   1</u> Make a copy of Practice Exercise 3 and attach it to a knot-free piece of pine or similar wood.

<u>Step   2</u> Review the four "Getting Started" steps on page 24.

<u>Step   3</u> Stand or sit directly <u>*in front of*</u> the saw. Relax and take a deep breath.

<u>Step   4</u> Using your fingertips only and a light touch, cut in as indicated. When you get to a sharp point on the object, instead of trying to make the sharp turn, cut past the object and loop back and around as indicated by the arrow heads (see figure 3).

<u>Step   5</u> When you have the project completely cut out, check the edges. You should have a continuous, smooth surface all around the fish with sharp exterior points at "A," "B," "C," "D" and "E."

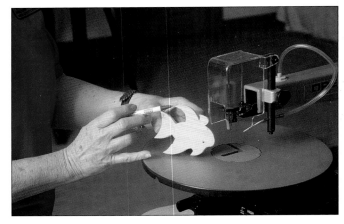

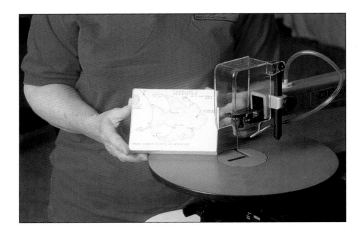

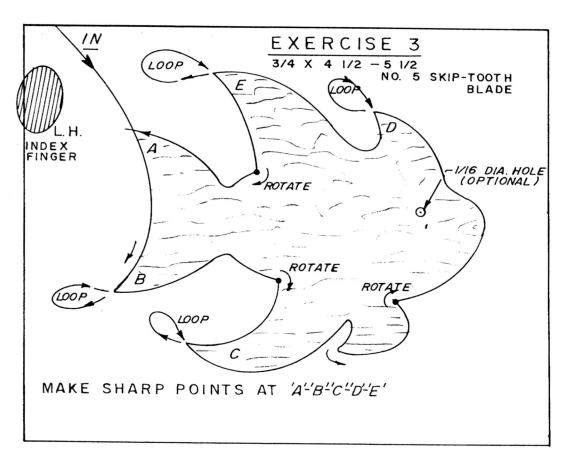

EXERCISE 3
3/4 X 4 1/2 — 5 1/2
NO. 5 SKIP-TOOTH BLADE

IN

LOOP

E

LOOP

D

L.H. INDEX FINGER

A

ROTATE

—1/16 DIA. HOLE (OPTIONAL)

B

LOOP

ROTATE

ROTATE

LOOP

C

MAKE SHARP POINTS AT 'A'-'B'-'C'-'D'-'E'

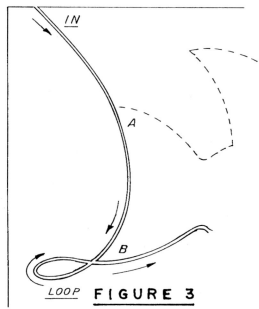

IN

A

B

LOOP FIGURE 3

PATTERN

Objective: To make interior cuts with sharp corners.

Materials needed:
(1) 3/4" x 4 1/2" - 5 1/2" long piece of wood
#5 skip tooth blade
1/8"-diameter drill

Step 1 Make a copy of Practice Exercise 4 and attach it to a knot-free piece of pine.

Step 2 Drill eight 1/8"-diameter starter holes as indicated. Lightly sand the back surface to remove any burrs from drilling holes.

Step 3 Review the four "Getting Started" steps on page 24.

Note: It is usually good practice to make all interior cuts first. This gives you more material to hold on to while making cuts.

Note: When making interior cuts, always try to cut so the blade cuts into a corner (see figures 4 and 5). This will make sharp corners.

Step 4 Stand or sit directly _in front of_ the saw. Relax and take a deep breath.

Step 5 Feed the blade into a starter hole. Re-tighten the blade and make the interior cut just as you would any exterior cut. Try to make good sharp corners.

Step 6 Continue making the remaining interior cuts. Note: Use the "loop" trick in making interior cuts to produce sharp interior corners. (See #1 of figure 5.)

Step 7 Make the final exterior cut. Use the "loop" method to make the sharp points on the wings.

Step 8 Check that all the interior cuts are sharp and that you have a continuous, smooth exterior cut. If you are not satisfied, repeat steps 1 through 7 on a new piece of wood.

FIRST CUT

CUT OUT **1st Cut**
Front starter hole,
cut to corner.

REMOVE PIECE

CUT OUT SECOND CUT
2nd Cut
Back to starter hole,
FIGURE 4 cut to corner

THIRD CUT

END

CUT OUT
3rd Cut
Back to starter hole
and cut remaining area.

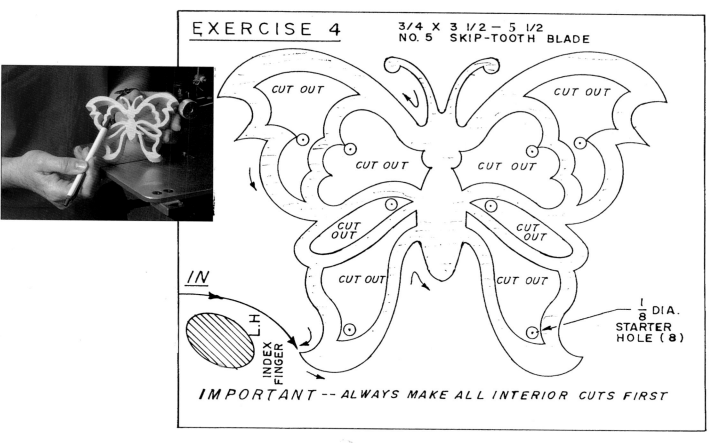

EXERCISE 4   3/4 X 3 1/2 — 5 1/2
NO. 5 SKIP-TOOTH BLADE

CUT OUT

CUT OUT   CUT OUT

CUT
OUT   CUT
                 OUT

CUT OUT   CUT OUT

IN

L.H.

INDEX FINGER

1/8 DIA.
STARTER
HOLE (8)

IMPORTANT -- ALWAYS MAKE ALL INTERIOR CUTS FIRST

PATTERN

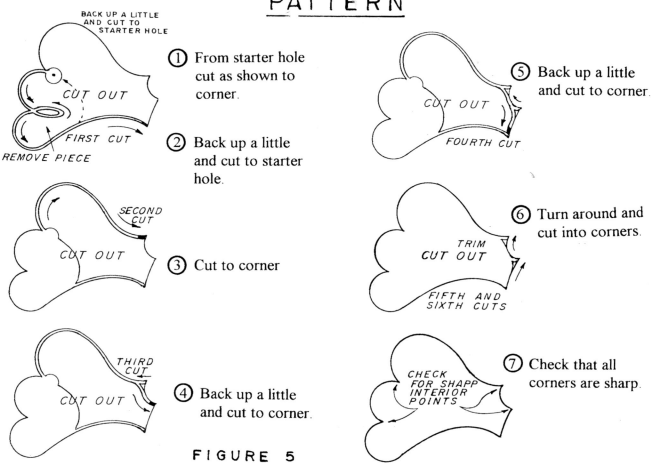

BACK UP A LITTLE
AND CUT TO
STARTER HOLE

CUT OUT

FIRST CUT

REMOVE PIECE

① From starter hole cut as shown to corner.

② Back up a little and cut to starter hole.

SECOND CUT

CUT OUT

③ Cut to corner

THIRD CUT

CUT OUT

④ Back up a little and cut to corner.

CUT OUT

FOURTH CUT

⑤ Back up a little and cut to corner.

TRIM
CUT OUT

FIFTH AND
SIXTH CUTS

⑥ Turn around and cut into corners.

CHECK
FOR SHAPP
INTERIOR
POINTS

⑦ Check that all corners are sharp.

FIGURE 5

Objective: To cut a very small object (Practice Exercise A) and a very thin object (Practice Exercise B).

Practice Exercise B

Practice Exercise A

Materials needed:

(1) 1/4" x 1³/4" - 2" wood (A)
(1) 4¹/2" x 5¹/2" piece of cardboard (A)
(1) ¹/16" x 3¹/2" - 4¹/2" wood (B)
(1) 4¹/2" X 5¹/2" piece of cardboard (B)
#2 skip tooth blade
¹/8"-diameter drill

Step 1 Make a copy of Practice Exercises 5A and 5B.

Step 2 Review the four "Getting Started" steps on page 24.

Step 3 For both exercises, glue the pattern to a piece of wood. Temporarily attach the wood to a piece of cardboard using rubber cement, a glue stick or masking tape. Use just enough adhesive to hold the wood to the cardboard while cutting out the object. The cardboard will help to keep your fingers away from the blade and give you better control over the movement of the wood.

Step 4 Stand or sit directly *in front of* the saw. Relax and take a deep breath.

Step 5 Make the cuts for the duck or the dog as you would any interior or exterior cut. Follow the arrows. Don't forget to use your fingertips and a light touch. *Relax!*

Step 6 Carefully remove the object from the cardboard and lightly sand the surface.

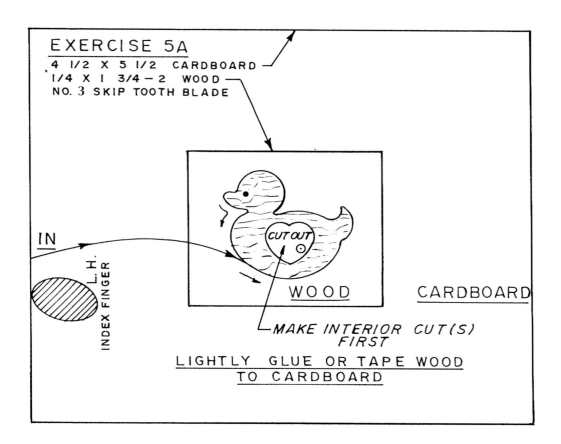

EXERCISE 5A
4 1/2 X 5 1/2 CARDBOARD
1/4 X 1 3/4 - 2 WOOD
NO. 3 SKIP TOOTH BLADE

IN

L. H. INDEX FINGER

CUT OUT

WOOD   CARDBOARD

MAKE INTERIOR CUT(S) FIRST

LIGHTLY GLUE OR TAPE WOOD TO CARDBOARD

PATTERN

EXERCISE 5 B
4 1/2 X 5 1/2 CARDBOARD
1/32 OR 1/16 X 3 1/2 - 4 1/2
NO. 3 SKIP-TOOTH BLADE

1/16 DIA. HOLE (OPTIONAL)

IN

L. H. INDEX FINGER

MASKING TAPE

PATTERN

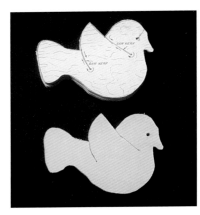

Objective: **To cut more than one object at the same time using the same pattern (stack cutting) using the STAPLE METHOD.**

Materials:
(3) 1/4" x 4 1/2" - 5 1/2" long piece of wood
#5 skip tooth blade
3/16" to 1/4" long staples
1/8"-diameter drill

Step   1 Make a copy of Practice Exercise 6.

Step   2 Staple the edges of three (3) 1/4"-thick pieces of wood together (see figure 6).

Step   3 Attach the pattern to the top of the stack. (See figure 6).

Step   4 Review the four "Getting Started" steps on page 24.

Step   5 Stand or sit directly *in front of* the saw. Relax and take a deep breath.

Step   6 Drill the 1/8"-diameter hole for the eye. Make the cuts for the bird as you would any exterior cut. Make a continuous, smooth flowing cut. Follow the arrows.

Step   7 When you are finished cutting out, remove the pattern and separate the objects. They all should be the same size and shape.

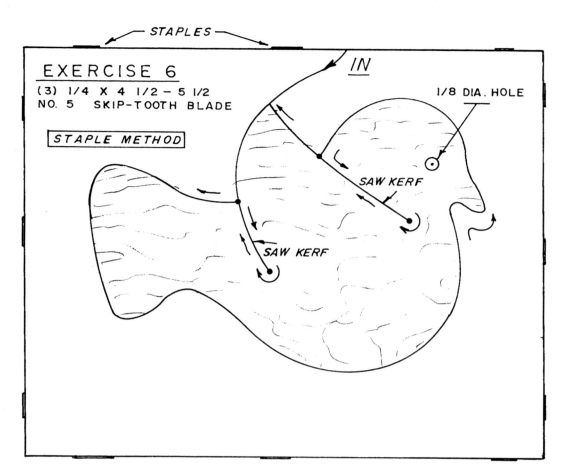

EXERCISE 6
(3) 1/4 X 4 1/2 – 5 1/2
NO. 5 SKIP-TOOTH BLADE

STAPLE METHOD

STAPLES

IN

1/8 DIA. HOLE

SAW KERF

SAW KERF

PATTERN

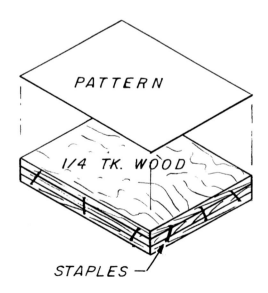

PATTERN

1/4 TK. WOOD

STAPLES

STAPLE METHOD

FIGURE 6

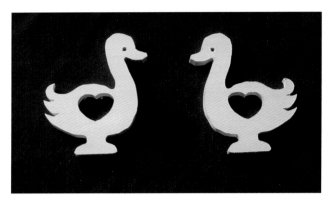

Objective: **To cut more than one object at the same time using the same pattern (stack cutting) using the TAPE METHOD.**

Materials:
(2) $1/2$" x $41/2$" - $51/2$" long piece of wood
#5 skip tooth blade
masking tape
$1/8$" diameter drill

Step 1 Make a copy of Practice Exercise 7.

Step 2 Stack the five pieces of wood and tape around the perimeter (see figure 7).

Step 3 Attach the pattern to the top piece of wood (see figure 7).

Step 4 Drill the hole for the eye with the $1/16$"-diameter drill. Drill the starter hole with the $1/8$"-diameter drill.

Step 5 Review the four "Getting Started" steps on page 24.

Step 6 Stand or sit directly _behind_ the saw. Relax and take a deep breath.

Step 7 Make the cuts for this project like you would any project with just a single piece of wood. Make continuous, smooth, flowing cuts with sharp corners and points.

Step 8 When you are finished cutting out, remove the pattern and separate the objects.

EXERCISE 7
(2) 1/2 X 4 1/2 — 5 1/2
NO. 5 SKIP-TOOTH BLADE
MASKING TAPE

MASKING TAPE

MASKING TAPE METHOD

1/8 DIA. HOLE

LOOPS

STARTER HOLE
CUT OUT

IN

PATTERN

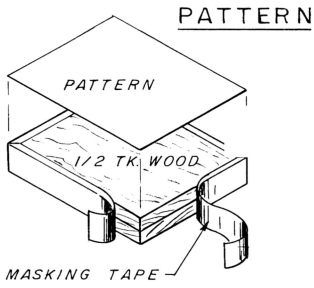

PATTERN

1/2 TK. WOOD

MASKING TAPE —

MASKING TAPE METHOD

FIGURE 7

Objective: To practice following straight lines and wavy lines, making sharp corners and turning in place, using the **BRAD METHOD.**

Materials needed:
(6) ¹/₈" x 4¹/₂" - 5¹/₂" long piece of wood
#5 skip tooth blade
(3) small brads
¹/₁₆"-diameter drill

Step   1   Make a copy of Practice Exercise 8.

Step   2   Stack the three pieces of wood and attach the pattern to the top of the stack.

Step   3   Add three or four small brads (as small as possible) outside the pattern lines at points "A," "B" and "C." (See figure 8.)

Step   4   Review the four "Getting Started" steps on page 24.

Step   5   Stand or sit directly *in front of* the saw. Relax and take a deep breath.

Step   6   Make the cuts as you would any exterior cut. Make a continuous, smooth, flowing cut.

Step   7   When finished cutting, remove the pattern and separate the objects.

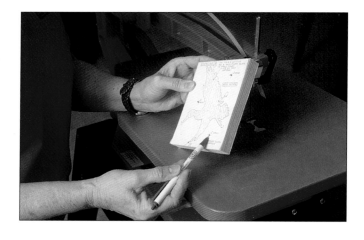

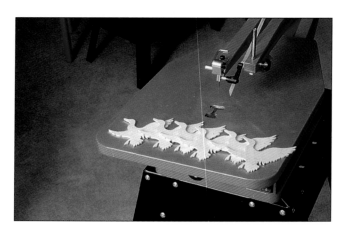

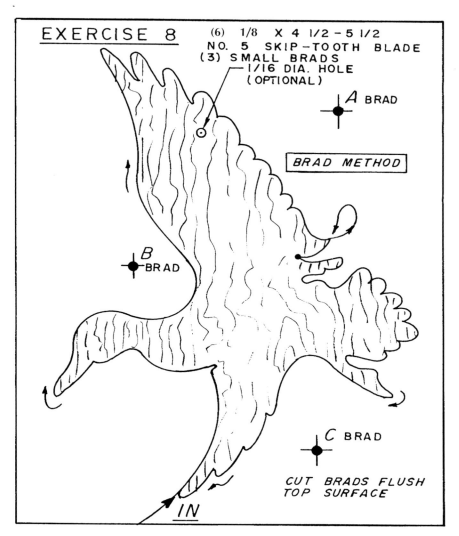

EXERCISE 8

(6) 1/8 X 4 1/2 – 5 1/2
NO. 5 SKIP–TOOTH BLADE
(3) SMALL BRADS
1/16 DIA. HOLE
(OPTIONAL)

A BRAD

BRAD METHOD

B BRAD

C BRAD

CUT BRADS FLUSH
TOP SURFACE

IN

PATTERN

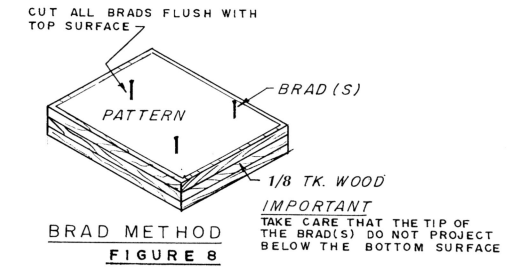

CUT ALL BRADS FLUSH WITH
TOP SURFACE

BRAD (S)

PATTERN

1/8 TK. WOOD

IMPORTANT
TAKE CARE THAT THE TIP OF
THE BRAD(S) DO NOT PROJECT
BELOW THE BOTTOM SURFACE

BRAD METHOD
FIGURE 8

Objective: To practice following straight and wavy lines, making sharp corners and turning in place using the EAR METHOD.

Materials needed:
(6) ¹/₈" x 4¹/₂" - 5¹/₂" long piece of wood
#5 skip tooth blade
(2) small brads

Step 1 Make a copy of Practice Exercise 9.

Step 2 Draw two or three "ears" on the outside edge of your pattern. (See the pattern for placement.) Try to space the ears out as far as possible. Stack the three pieces of wood and attach the pattern to the top of the stack.

Step 3 Stack the pieces and add small brads in the center of each "ear." (See figure 9.)

Step 4 Stand or sit directly _in front of_ the saw. Relax and take a deep breath.

Step 5 Review the four "Getting Started" steps on page 24.

Step 6 Make cuts as you would for any exterior cut. Make a continuous, smooth, flowing cut. Be sure <u>not</u> to cut off the "ears" at this time.

Step 7 When you have finished cutting out the pattern, keep the three pieces of wood, with the "ears" and brads still attached, together.

Step 8 Hold the pieces tightly and carefully cut off the ears.

NOTE: There are other methods, or even combinations of methods to stack cut that will work just as well as the staple, tape, brad and ear methods. You could use rubber cement or double-faced masking tape to temporarily hold the pieces together, or use a hot glue gun to glue areas <u>outside</u> the pattern. We recommend that you don't stack more than 1¹/₂" to 1³/₄ of thick material to cut.

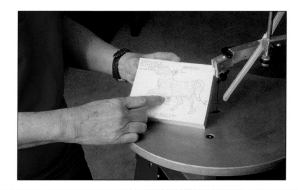

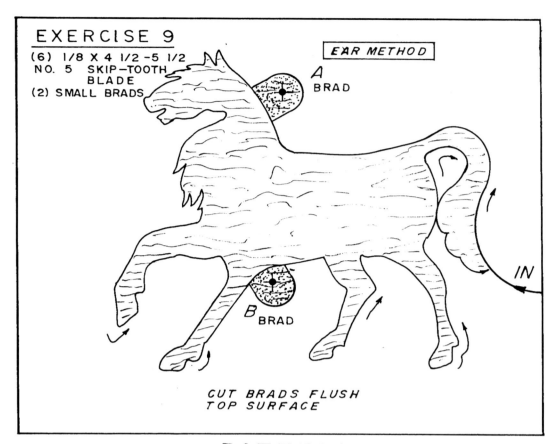

EXERCISE 9
(6) 1/8 X 4 1/2 -5 1/2
NO. 5 SKIP—TOOTH
BLADE
(2) SMALL BRADS

EAR METHOD

A BRAD

B BRAD

IN

CUT BRADS FLUSH
TOP SURFACE

PATTERN

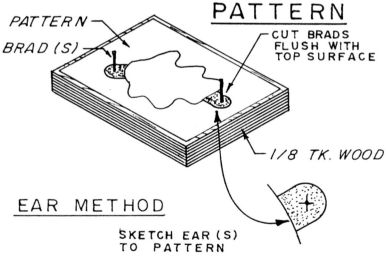

PATTERN

BRAD (S)

CUT BRADS
FLUSH WITH
TOP SURFACE

1/8 TK. WOOD

EAR METHOD

SKETCH EAR (S)
TO PATTERN

FIGURE 9

Objective: **To cut paper, cardboard or cloth (exterior cut).**

Materials:
(2) $1/8$" x $41/4$" - $51/2$" plywood
10 sheets of $81/2$" x 11 paper (cut into four $41/4$" x $51/2$" pieces. 20 total)
#5 skip toothblade
$3/4$" inch wide masking tape
$1/16$"-diameter drill

Step 1 Make a copy of Practice Exercise 10.

Step 2 Sandwich the 20 sheets of paper between the two $1/8$"-thick pieces of plywood. Line up the edges. (See figure 10.)

Step 3 Tape all four edges using $3/4$"-wide masking tape. Next spray the pattern with adhesive and attach the pattern to the *top* piece of plywood.

Step 4 Drill the two $1/16$"-diameter holes.

Step 5 Review the four "Getting Started" steps on page 24.

Step 6 Stand or sit directly *in front of* the saw. Relax and take a deep breath.

Step 7 Make the exterior cuts. Be sure to make the entire cut without cutting out to the edge. Don't forget, the masking tape is holding everything together.

NOTE: Any stack cutting method will work. If the masking tape method is not functional, use one of the other stack cutting methods. (This method is great if you make quilts. Simply cut the cloth to the overall size, iron them and sandwich the pieces between the plywood as you would paper, then cut out. (Note: The scroll saw will not cut felt.)

Step 8 When you are finished cutting out the project, remove all 20 pieces of paper. All of the pieces should match.

NOTE: Cutting paper or cardboard dulls your scroll saw blade very quickly. Your blade will probably need to be replaced when you have finished cutting out this project.

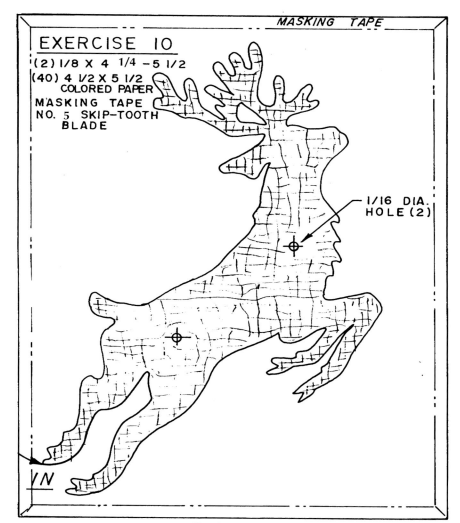

EXERCISE 10
(2) 1/8 X 4 1/4 – 5 1/2
(40) 4 1/2 X 5 1/2
COLORED PAPER
MASKING TAPE
NO. 5 SKIP-TOOTH
BLADE

1/16 DIA.
HOLE (2)

IN

PATTERN

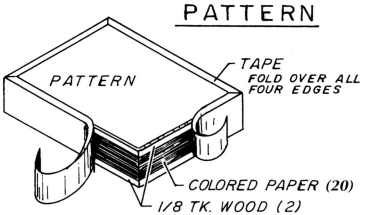

PATTERN

TAPE
FOLD OVER ALL
FOUR EDGES

COLORED PAPER (20)

1/8 TK. WOOD (2)

FIGURE 10

Objective: To cut paper, cloth or cardboard (interior cut).

Materials:
(2) 1/8" x 5 - 8¹/₂" long sheets of plywood
40 sheets of 8¹/₂ x 11" paper
³/₄"-wide masking tape

Step 1 Make a copy of Practice Exercise 11.

Step 2 Sandwich the 40 sheets of paper between the pieces of plywood. Line up the top edge and the two sides.

Step 3 Tape all four edges using ³/₄"-wide masking tape. Spray adhesive on the back of the pattern and attach the pattern to the top piece of plywood. (See figure 11.)

Step 4 Drill the three required starter holes.

Step 5 Review the four "Getting Started" steps on page 24.

Step 6 Stand or sit directly *in front of* the saw. Relax and take a deep breath.

Step 7 Make all of the interior cuts. Be sure to make good, sharp corners.

Step 8 When you are finished cutting out the project, carefully remove the masking tape and separate the pieces.

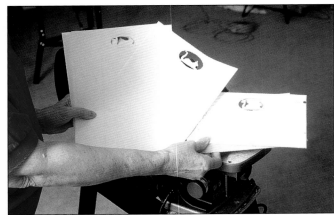

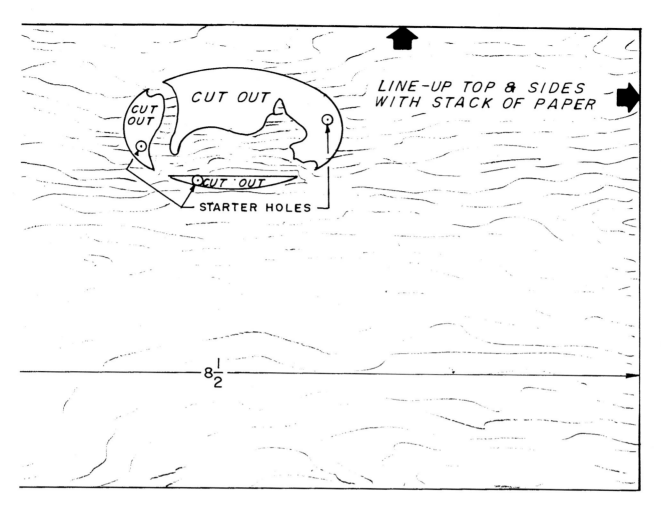

CUT OUT

CUT OUT

CUT OUT

STARTER HOLES

LINE-UP TOP & SIDES
WITH STACK OF PAPER

$8\frac{1}{2}$

PATTERN

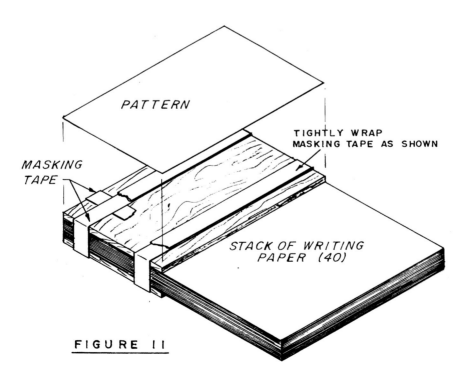

PATTERN

TIGHTLY WRAP
MASKING TAPE AS SHOWN

MASKING
TAPE

STACK OF WRITING
PAPER (40)

FIGURE II

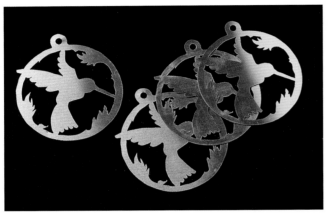

Objective: To cut metal (aluminum, brass or steel).

Materials needed:
(2) $1/8$" x $41/2$" - $51/2$" sheets of plywood
4 sheets of $41/2$" x $51/2$" aluminum flashing
   (obtained from any local building supply company — cut to size with scissors)
#3 scroll saw blade
$3/4$" masking tape
$1/8$"-diameter drill
$1/4$"-diameter drill

Step 1 Make a copy of Practice Exercise 12.

Step 2 Sandwich the four sheets of aluminum between the pieces of plywood. Line up all of the edges.

Step 3 Tape all four edges using $3/4$"-wide masking tape (see figure 12). Attach the pattern to the top piece of plywood.

Step 4 Drill the four required starter holes with the $1/8$" drill. Drill the $1/4$"-diameter hole at the top.

Step 5 Review the four "Getting Started" steps on page 24.

Step 6 Stand or sit directly *in front of* the saw. Relax and take a deep breath.

Step 7 Make all the interior cuts. Keep good, sharp interior corners as you would if you were cutting wood.

Step 8 Make the exterior cut. Make the entire cut at one time without cutting out to the edge. Don't forget, the masking tape is holding everything together. Note: Any stack cutting method can be used. If the masking tape method is not functional for a particular project, use one of the other stack cutting methods in the previous exercises.

NOTE: The plywood keeps the blade cool. You might want to slow your saw down a little, especially if you are cutting brass or steel. Some people add a little oil to the blade as they cut, but I find this messy.

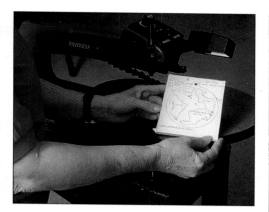

EXERCISE 12

(2) 1/8 X 4 1/2 -5 1/2
(4) 4 1/2 X 5 1/2
    ALUMINUM FLASHING
NO. 3 SKIP-TOOTH
       BLADE
TAPE

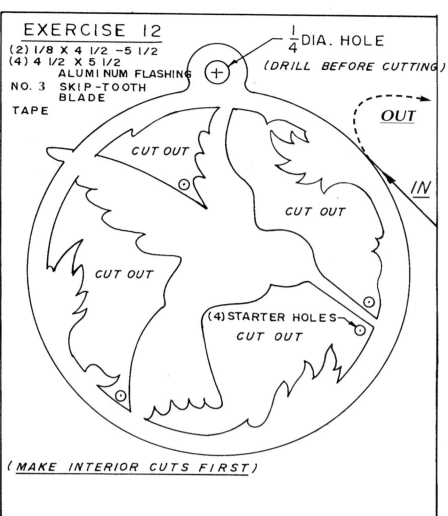

¼ DIA. HOLE
(DRILL BEFORE CUTTING)

OUT

IN

CUT OUT

CUT OUT

CUT OUT

(4) STARTER HOLES
CUT OUT

(MAKE INTERIOR CUTS FIRST)

PATTERN

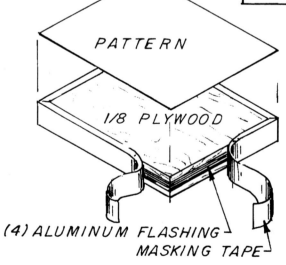

PATTERN

1/8 PLYWOOD

(4) ALUMINUM FLASHING
    MASKING TAPE

FIGURE 12

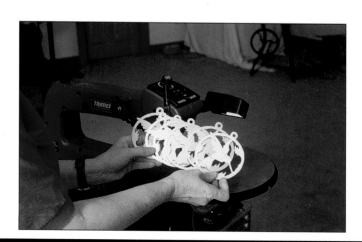

<u>**Objective:**</u> **To cut plastic or Plexiglas®.**

<u>**Materials needed:**</u>
(3) $1/8$" inch x $41/2$" - $51/2$" pieces of plastic or Plexiglas®
#5 crown tooth blade or a standard #5 blade
$3/4$"-wide masking tape
2"-wide duct tape

Step 1 Make a copy of Practice Exercise 13.

Step 2 Plastic cuts just like plywood, but most plastic melts back together as you cut through it. To prevent this, apply strips of 2"-wide duct tape to the top surface of each piece of plastic or Plexiglas®. Try not to leave any spaces or overlap the duct tape.

Step 3 Tape all 3 pieces of plastic or Plexiglas® together (see figure 13).

Step 4 Attach the pattern copy over the top sheet of plastic and on top of the duct tape.

Step 5 Stand or sit directly _in front of_ the saw. Relax and take a deep breath.

Step 6 Cut out the project as you would any regular project in wood.

NOTE: $1/8$"-inch thick plastic is a great material for stack cutting. Most plastic or Plexiglas® comes with a thin protective piece of paper or plastic over the top surface. Put the duct tape right over the protective membrane. This will make it easy to remove the duct tape after cutting out your project.

TIP: If you have to put duct tape on the bottom of the plastic or Plexiglas®, glue a plain sheet of paper over the duct tape. The duct tape "drags" as you are cutting and making turns on your project; the paper will eliminate the "drag."

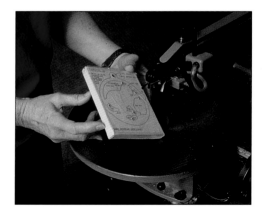

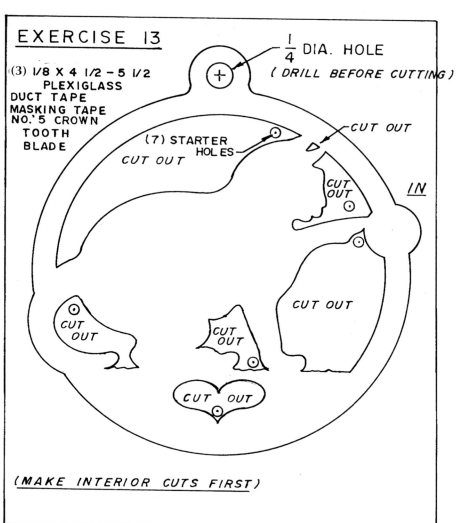

EXERCISE 13

(3) 1/8 X 4 1/2 - 5 1/2
PLEXIGLASS
DUCT TAPE
MASKING TAPE
NO. 5 CROWN
TOOTH
BLADE

1/4 DIA. HOLE
(DRILL BEFORE CUTTING)

(7) STARTER HOLES

CUT OUT

CUT OUT

CUT OUT

CUT OUT

CUT OUT

CUT OUT

CUT OUT

IN

(MAKE INTERIOR CUTS FIRST)

PATTERN

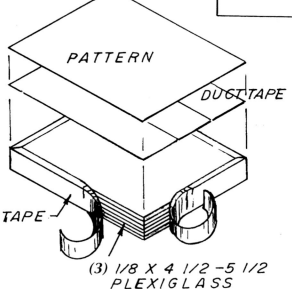

PATTERN

DUCT TAPE

TAPE

(3) 1/8 X 4 1/2 -5 1/2
PLEXIGLASS

FIGURE 13

Objective: **To study the basics of relief cutting and to make a Relief Cut Blade/Angle Tester for future reference.**

Materials needed:
(1) 3/4" x 41/2" - 7 long piece of pine
#5 skip tooth blade

Step 1 Make a copy of Practice Exercise 14 and attach it to a knot-free piece of pine or similar wood.

Step 2 Cut the wood in half along the dotted line

Step 3 Carefully, set the saw table at a 21/2 degree angle, _left side down_. (If you have a saw that doesn't tip to the left, tilt your table to the right, but cut in the _opposite_ direction of the arrows on all projects.)

Step 4 Stand or sit directly _in front of_ the saw. Relax and take a deep breath.

Step 5 Carefully, make one clockwise cut and one counter-clockwise cut at 21/2" where indicated. Save the pieces. Make sure they are marked and kept in order for further use.

Step 6 Set your saw table at 31/2 degrees, _left side down._

Step 7 Carefully, make one clockwise cut and one counter-clockwise cut at 31/2"where indicated. Save the pieces. Mark them and keep them in order.

Step 8 Now, set your saw table at 41/2 degrees, _left side down._

Step 9 Carefully, make one clockwise cut and one counter-clockwise cut at 41/2" where indicated. Save the pieces. Mark them and keep them in order.

Step 10 Set your saw table at 51/2 degrees, _left side down._

Step 11 Carefully, make one clockwise cut and one counter clockwise cut at 51/2" where indicated. Save the pieces. Mark them and keep them in order.

Step 12 Re-position all of the pieces and push or pull them until they are snug. You will find the 21/2 degree pieces _almost_ come through. The 51/2 degree pieces project in or out very little.

Step 13 From the back, glue the eight cut-out pieces in place.

Step 14 Keep this tester handy for various relief cutting projects.

Step 15 Keep the other side to make a tester using another size of blade.

NOTE: With the table top <u>left side down</u>, pieces cut in a clockwise direction at various angles will go <u>in away from you.</u> If you cut in a counter-clockwise direction at various angles, the pieces will come <u>out toward you.</u>

NOTE: This is your Relief Cut Blade/Angle Tester. Keep it handy for future reference. It will show you what happens if you use 3/4"-thick wood cut at 2¹/₂, 3¹/₂, 4¹/₂ or 5¹/₂ degrees in a clockwise or counter-clockwise direction using a #5 blade. If any one of the three variables change, you will get different results. If you are doing a project with a different thickness and a different saw blade number, make a new Tester and note on it the size of the blade you used.

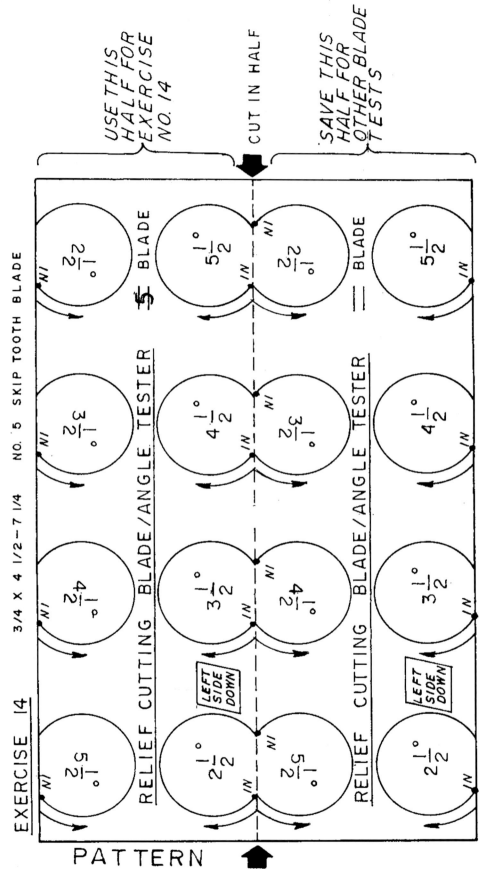

Objective: **To practice relief cutting to make a collapsible basket.**

Materials needed:
(1) $3/4$" x $8 1/2$" - $12 1/2$" long piece of hardwood (maple, birch, cherry, oak)
#5 skip tooth blade
$1/8$" diameter drill
$1/32$" diameter drill
Router with $1/4$" radius round over bit (optional)

Step 1 Make a copy of the two halves of the pattern.

Step 2 Line up the two halves of the pattern and glue them together (the areas marked "X" should match up) to get a full pattern.

Step 3 Glue the pattern to the wood.

Step 4 Drill all 10 starter holes with a $1/8$" diameter drill; then make all the interior cuts in the top half.

Step 5 Review the four "Getting Started" steps on page 24.

Step 6 Stand or sit directly *in front of* the saw. Relax and take a deep breath.

Step 7 Make the exterior cut.

Step 8 Drill five $1/16$"-diameter holes as noted. Be sure to get all five holes "a," "b," "c", "d" and "e."

Step 9 Cut the round basket frame, starting at hole "a" and remove the basket.

Step 10 Cut out the foot detail (bottom) of the basket.

Step 11 Using a router and a $1/4$" radius round over follower bit, round the top and bottom edges of the basket frame. If you don't have a router, simply sand the top and bottom edges of the basket frame to get a rounded edge on the top and the bottom.

Step 12 Set the saw table to 4 degrees, <u>left side down.</u>

Step 13 Start at starter hole "b" on the basket frame and cut clockwise as shown around to the end of the spiral.

Step 14 Re-set saw at 0 degrees. *This is important*!

Step 15 Carefully, add three small brads or three small #4 flat head wood screws at the two side pivot points and the foot. Make sure that the foot swivels.

Step 16 Sand all over.

Step 17 Finish to suit.

NOTE: If the basket does <u>not</u> extend down to the bottom of the opening and lock in place, you will have to make another basket setting the angle of the table at $3 1/2$ degrees to 3 degrees. The smaller the degree the more the basket will drop.

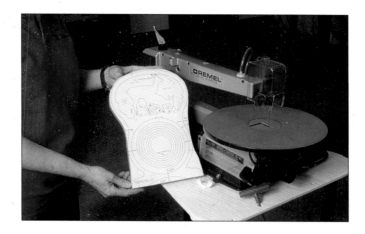

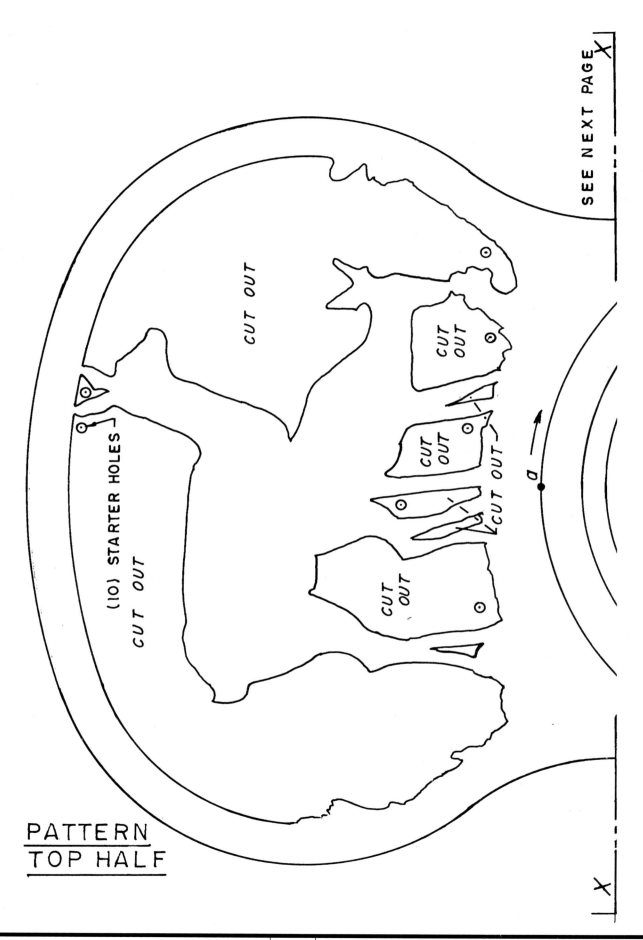

PATTERN
TOP HALF

(10) STARTER HOLES

CUT OUT

CUT OUT

CUT OUT

CUT OUT

CUT OUT

CUT OUT

CUT OUT

a

X

X

SEE NEXT PAGE

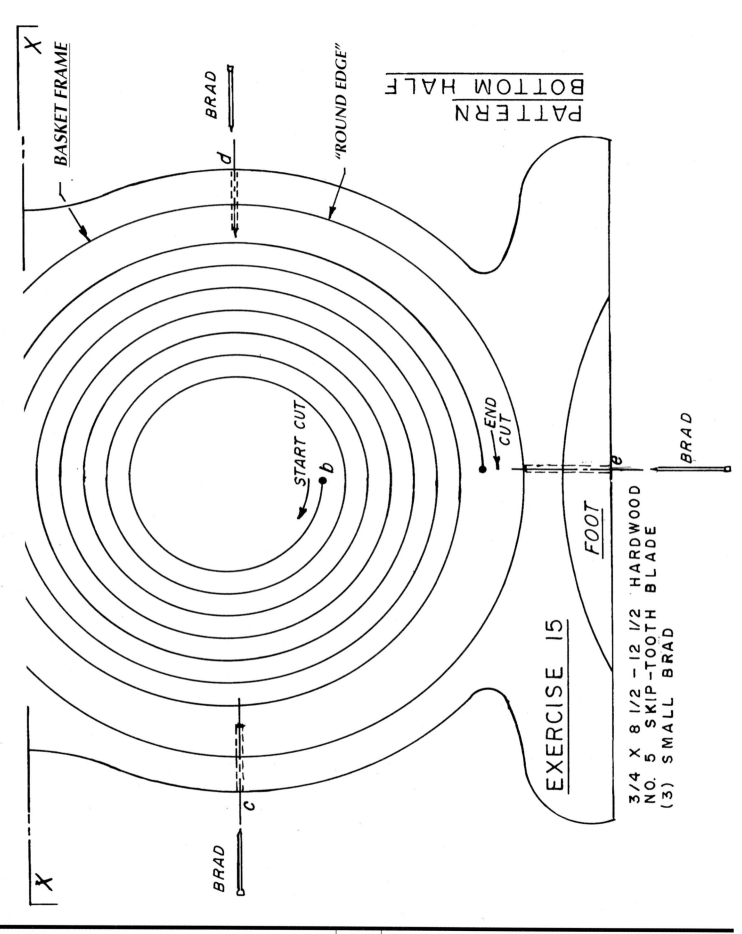

BASKET FRAME

X

BRAD

d

"ROUND EDGE"

PATTERN
BOTTOM HALF

START CUT

b

END CUT

e

BRAD

FOOT

EXERCISE 15

3/4 X 8 1/2 – 12 1/2 HARDWOOD
NO. 5 SKIP-TOOTH BLADE
(3) SMALL BRAD

c

BRAD

X

BRAD

Objective: **To illustrate how to get a dimensional effect using relief cutting.**

Materials needed:
(1) ³/₄" x 4¹/₂" - 5¹/₂" piece of wood
#5 skip tooth blade

Step 1 Make a copy of Practice Exercise 16 and attach it to a knot-free piece of pine or similar wood.

Step 2 Set your saw table at 3 degrees, _left side down_.

Step 3 Review the four "Getting Started" steps on page 24.

Step 4 Stand or sit directly _in front of_ the saw. Relax and take a deep breath.

Step 5 Cutting in a counter-clockwise direction, cut out the cat (Cut #1).

Step 6 Cutting in a clockwise direction, cut out the door way (Cut #2).

Step 7 Cutting in a counter-clockwise direction, cut out the house (Cut #3). Be sure to make all of the tight turns in place, do not loop out and around.

NOTE: If your saw does not tilt to the left, tilt it to the right and make all of the cuts opposite the direction indicated.

NOTE: Compare the results of the cat door and house with your Relief Cut Blade/Angle Tester (Practice Exercise 14).
1. All cuts from left to right will bring the area <u>out</u>.
2. All cuts from right to left will move the area <u>in</u>.
3. The smaller the angle degree the further <u>in</u> or <u>out</u> the surface will extend.

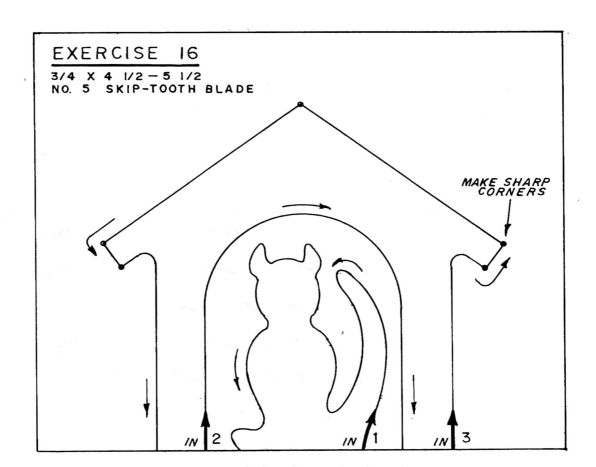

EXERCISE 16

3/4 X 4 1/2 — 5 1/2
NO. 5 SKIP-TOOTH BLADE

MAKE SHARP CORNERS

IN 2   IN 1   IN 3

PATTERN

Objective: **To study the basics of inlay work and to make an Inlay Blade/Angle Tester for future reference.**

Materials needed:
(1) 1/4" x 31/4" - 81/8" dark wood (walnut)*
(1) 1/4" x 31/4" - 81/8" light wood (maple)*
#3 skip tooth blade
1/4"-thick masking tape.
        *Important: Both pieces of wood must be exactly the same thickness.

Step 1 Make a copy of Practice Exercise 17.

Note: This is a test piece, using a #3 blade.
        There are three factors involved in inlay work:
        1. Thickness of wood.
        2. Thickness of the scroll saw blade.
        3. Angle of table tilt.
        If you change any one of the above factors your results will differ from those in this practice exercise. Inlay is an extension of relief cutting.

Step 2 Decide which wood will be the base (background) and which will be the design (pattern). If you want a dark base or background, the dark piece of wood should be placed on top. If you want a light base or background, place the light piece of wood on top.

Step 3 Assuming you want a light background with a dark pattern, tape the two pieces together with the light wood on top and the dark wood on the bottom.

Step 4 Attach the pattern to the top piece of wood. (See figure 15.)

Step 5 Review the four "Getting Started" steps on page 24.

Step 6 Set your saw at a 1/2 degree angle, *left side down.*

Step 7 Stand or sit directly *in front of* the saw. Relax and take a deep breath.

Step 8 Make the first cut, counter-clockwise as indicated. Number the pieces and save the dark-colored bottom piece.

Step 9 Set your saw at 1 degree, *left side down.*

Step 10 Make the second cut counter-clockwise as indicated. Number the pieces and save the dark-colored bottom piece.

Step 11 Set your saw at 11/2 degrees, *left side down.*

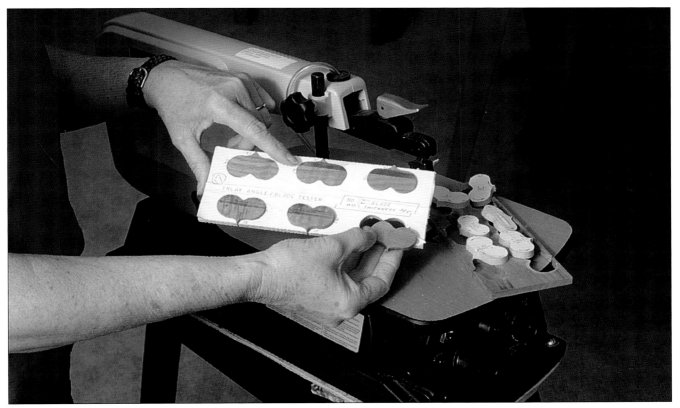

Step 12 Make the third cut counter-clockwise as indicated. Number the pieces and save the dark-colored bottom piece.

Step 13 Set your saw at 2 degrees, *left side down.*

Step 14 Make the fourth cut counter-clockwise as indicated. Number the pieces and save the dark-colored bottom piece.

Step 15 Set your saw at 2¹/₂ degrees, *left side down.*

Step 16 Make the fifth cut counter-clockwise as indicated. Number the pieces and save the dark-colored bottom piece.

Step 17 Set your saw at 3 degrees, *left side down.*

Step 18 Make the sixth cut counter-clockwise as indicated. Number the pieces and save the dark-colored bottom piece.

Step 19 Separate the two ¹/₄" thick pieces. Discard the dark-colored bottom piece; the light-colored piece will be the background. Remove the paper pattern.

Step 20 Place each of the 6 pieces back into their exact places. Note: You will be using the light-colored top piece as the *background*. You will be trying to put the dark-colored pieces into the *light* piece.

Step 21 Only one, possibly two pieces will fit into the hole in the background exactly. For the inlay you want a snug, but not too tight fit. The top and bottom (light and dark) pieces should line up and actually stay in place with out gluing them together.

NOTE: Using ¹/₄"-thick wood, a #3 skip tooth saw blade and the degree setting you found worked the best will always yield the same results.

Step 22 Glue the one piece that fits correctly in place. Save this Tester for future reference. This is your setting for ¹/₄"-thick material, using a #3 skip tooth blade.

Step 23 Sand the top and bottom surfaces - finish project to suit.

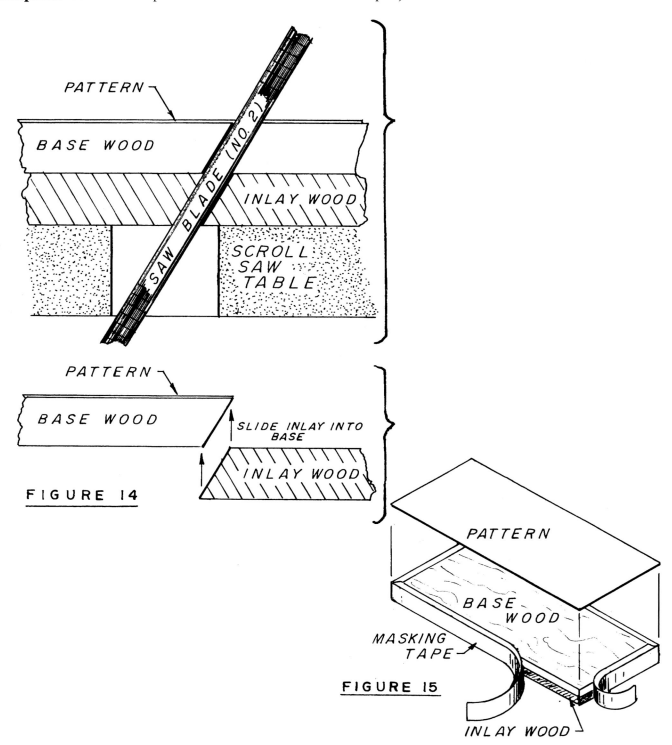

PATTERN

BASE WOOD

SAW BLADE (NO. 2)

INLAY WOOD

SCROLL SAW TABLE

PATTERN

BASE WOOD

SLIDE INLAY INTO BASE

INLAY WOOD

FIGURE 14

PATTERN

BASE WOOD

MASKING TAPE

FIGURE 15

INLAY WOOD

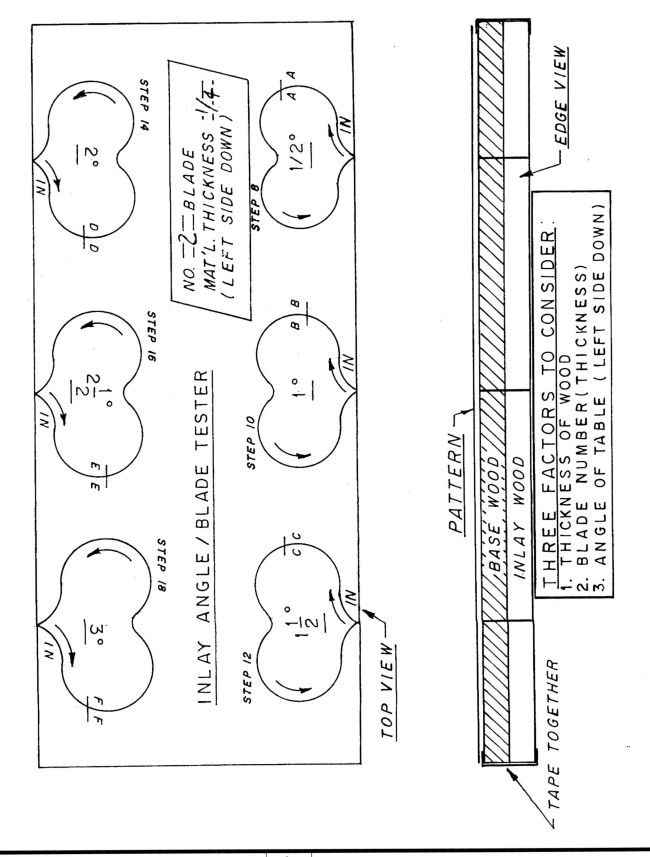

INLAY ANGLE / BLADE TESTER

NO. 2 BLADE
MAT'L. THICKNESS 1/4
(LEFT SIDE DOWN)

STEP 8
1/2°

STEP 10
1°

STEP 12
1 1/2°

STEP 14
2°

STEP 16
2 1/2°

STEP 18
3°

TOP VIEW

EDGE VIEW

PATTERN

BASE WOOD

INLAY WOOD

TAPE TOGETHER

THREE FACTORS TO CONSIDER:
1. THICKNESS OF WOOD
2. BLADE NUMBER (THICKNESS)
3. ANGLE OF TABLE (LEFT SIDE DOWN)

Objective: **To make an inlay practice project.**

Materials needed:
(1) 1/4" x 41/2" - 51/2" dark wood (walnut)*
(1) 1/4" x 41/2" - 51/2" light wood (maple)*
#3 skip tooth blade
3/4" masking tape
      ***Note:** Choose high contrasting woods for a dynamic
      effect.
1/32" diameter drill

Step   1 Make a copy of Practice Exercise 18.

Review: Remember, there are three factors to consider in inlay work.
    1. Thickness of wood.
    2. Thickness of blade.
    3. Angle of table top.
    We will use the same thickness of wood, the same size blade and the same table setting that worked best in the Inlay Blade/Angle Tester (Practice Exercise 17). Remember, when using this method, always cut in a counter-clockwise direction.

Step 2 Decide which wood will be the base (background) and which will be the design (inlay). In this example we will have a light background and dark inlay.

Step 3 Stack the two pieces of wood and tape them together with the light-colored background wood on top.

Step 4 Attach the pattern to the top piece of wood.

Step 5 Drill a small starter hole with a 1/32" diameter bit; the smaller the better. (If you do not have a very small drill bit, use a very <u>thin</u>, stiff wire in your drill press in place of the drill bit.)

Step 6 Set the scroll saw at whatever table top angle setting you found worked best in Practice Exercise 17, *left side down.*

Step 7 Insert the blade through the starter hole.

Step 8 Review the four "Getting Started" steps on page 24.

Step 9 Stand or sit directly *in front of* the saw. Relax and take a deep breath.

Step 10 Following the pattern exactly, make a smooth, continuous cut. Do <u>not</u> stray from the pattern and do not make any "loops" at the sharp turns.

Step 11 Remove the inlay from the dark-colored bottom piece and insert it into the light-colored top (background) piece. If everything is correct the inlay should fit snugly into the background as it did in the Inlay Blade/Angle Tester (Practice Exercise 17).

Step 12 Using very little glue, glue the inlay in place. Sand the top and bottom surfaces with the inlay in place.

Step 13 Finish to suit.

Note: The leftover pieces can not be used to make another relief project, but you can use the hummingbird cutout for another project if you wish.

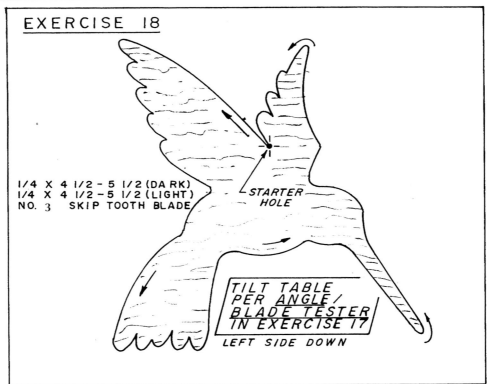

EXERCISE 18

1/4 X 4 1/2 - 5 1/2 (DARK)
1/4 X 4 1/2 - 5 1/2 (LIGHT)
NO. 3 SKIP TOOTH BLADE

STARTER HOLE

TILT TABLE PER ANGLE/ BLADE TESTER IN EXERCISE 17
LEFT SIDE DOWN

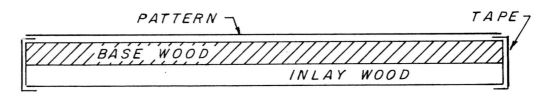

PATTERN

TAPE

BASE WOOD

INLAY WOOD

PATTERN

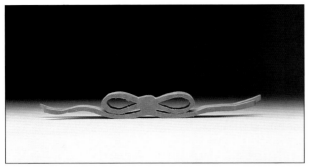

Objective: **To make a three dimensional project using the compound cutting method.**

Materials needed:
(1) 3/4" x 1" - 5¹/2" long piece of knot-free pine
#3 skip tooth blade.

Step   1 Make a copy of Practice Exercise 19.

Step   2 Compound cutting is simply making one cut in the top surface, turning the material (in this case wood) and making a second cut on front surface to create a three-dimensional project. First, fold the pattern along the fold line. Spray the pattern with an adhesive and attach the pattern to the wood on the two sides. (See figure 16.)

Step   3 Drill two small holes in the loops of the bow.

Step   4 Review the four "Getting Started" steps on page 24.

Step   5 Stand or sit directly _in front of_ the saw. Relax and take a deep breath.

Step   6 On the top, cut the two inside loops (first cut). Save the pieces.

Step   7 Make the second and third cut. Save the pieces.

Step   8 Using 3/4"-wide masking tape, tape everything back together.

Step   9 Turn the wood 90 degrees and cut out the front view profile (fourth cut).

Step 10 Remove all the pieces to expose the bow.

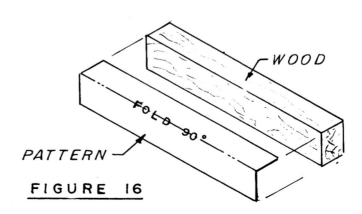

WOOD

FOLD 90°

PATTERN

FIGURE 16

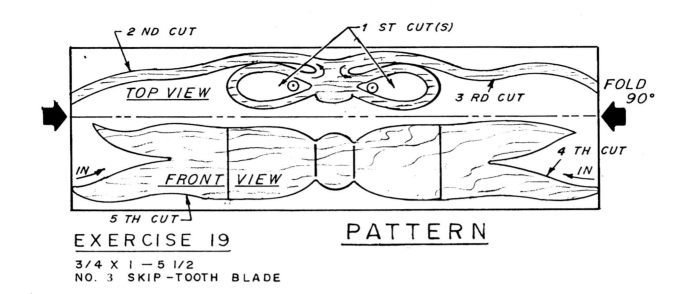

2 ND CUT

1 ST CUT(S)

TOP VIEW

3 RD CUT

FOLD 90°

IN

FRONT VIEW

4 TH CUT

IN

5 TH CUT

EXERCISE 19

PATTERN

3/4 X 1 — 5 1/2
NO. 3 SKIP-TOOTH BLADE

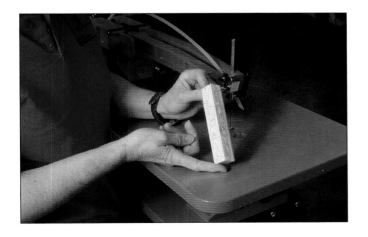

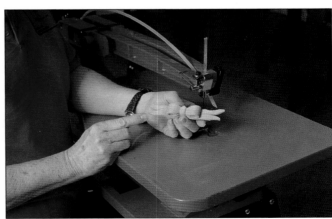

Objective: To practice layering to produce the illusion of a woven basket.

Materials needed:
(3) 1/4" x 31/4" - 53/4" light wood - Level A*
(3) 1/4" x 31/4" - 53/4" light wood - Level B*
(1) 3/16" x 31/4" - 53/4" dark wood - Bottom*
(1) 3/16" x 31/4" - 53/4" dark wood - Top*
(1) 3/8" x 3 - 31/4" dark wood - Handle*
#2 skip tooth blade
    *Cut wood to overall size; choose a softer hardwood such as aspen, boxwood or basswood.

Step   1   Make a copy of Practice Exercise 20.

Step   2   Stack the three Level A pieces and the three Level B pieces in two separate stacks. tape the Level A pieces and the Level B pieces together with masking tape.

Step   3   Using adhesive spray, attach the patterns for Level A and Level B to the top of their respective stacks.

Step   4   Drill a starter in the stack for Level A and Level B.

Step   5   Review the four "Getting Started" steps on page 24.

Step   6   Stand or sit directly _in front of_ the saw. Relax and take a deep breath.

Step   7   Carefully, cut out the interior section of Level A; make good tight turns.

Step   8   Make the external cut in Level A. Important: Keep the interior sections in place for support while making this cut. Again make good tight turns.

Step 9   Repeat steps 7, 8 and 9 to cut out Level B.

Step 10   With a pencil, add an alignment dot on each piece (Level A and Level B) for reference during assembly. Line up all the dots during assembly.

Step 11   Attach the patterns for the top rim and the base to the wood.

Step 12   Cut out the top rim and the base. Be sure the two notches in the top rim are the same thickness as the handle material.

Step 13   Attach the handle pattern to the wood.

Step 14   Cut out the handle.

Step 15 Sand all the pieces. Be sure to keep all the edges sharp.

Step 16 Fit the handle into the top rim and glue it in place.

Step 17 Place a series of a small dots of glue about two inches apart all around one piece of Level A. The line-up dot should be in the bottom left corner as shown.

Step 18 Using the dots as reference, center one piece of Level B over Level A and let the glue set.

Step 19 Place a series of small dots of glue about two inches apart all around Level B.

Step 20 Using the dots, center one piece of Level A over Level B and let the glue set.

Step 21 Keep adding Level B and Level A pieces, alternating them until all of the layers are in place. Keep everything square and centered. Don't forget to keep all line-up dots over each other.

Step 22 Center and glue the top rim with the handle to the "weave" section. Glue the base in place.

Step 23 Finish or leave unfinished.

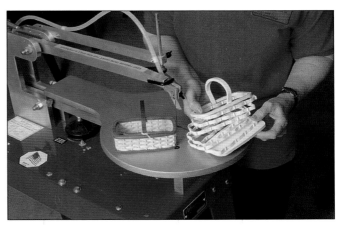

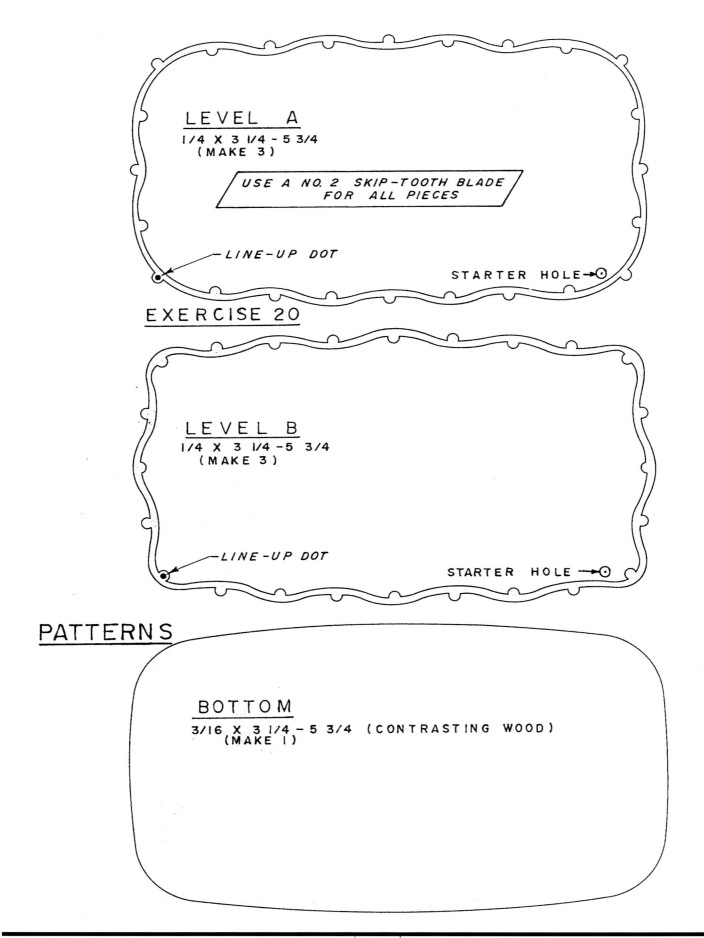

LEVEL A
1/4 X 3 1/4 - 5 3/4
(MAKE 3)

USE A NO. 2 SKIP-TOOTH BLADE
FOR ALL PIECES

—LINE-UP DOT

STARTER HOLE →⊙

EXERCISE 20

LEVEL B
1/4 X 3 1/4 - 5 3/4
(MAKE 3)

—LINE-UP DOT

STARTER HOLE →⊙

PATTERNS

BOTTOM
3/16 X 3 1/4 - 5 3/4 (CONTRASTING WOOD)
(MAKE 1)

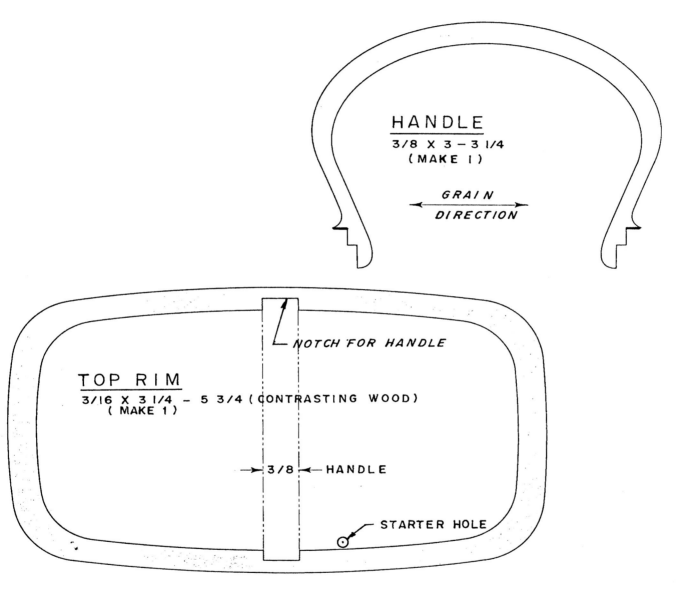

HANDLE
3/8 X 3 – 3 1/4
(MAKE 1)

GRAIN
DIRECTION

NOTCH FOR HANDLE

TOP RIM
3/16 X 3 1/4 – 5 3/4 (CONTRASTING WOOD)
(MAKE 1)

3/8 — HANDLE

STARTER HOLE

PATTERNS

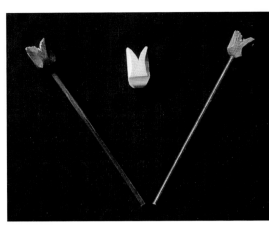

Objective: To make a simple tulip from scrap wood cut to size.

Materials needed:
(1) 3/4" x 3/4" - 5" length (minimum)
#5 skip tooth blade.

Step   1 Make a copy of Practice Exercise 21.

Step   2 Stand or sit directly _in front of_ the saw. Relax and take a deep breath.

Step   3 Make the first cut—two simple arc swings into the center—approximately 5/8" down.

Step   4 Rotate the board 90 degrees and make two simple arc swings into the center the same depth as in step 4.

Step   5 Set the saw table top at 45 degrees, _left side down._

Step   6 Make a simple arc. Cut 45 degrees from the tip to about 1" to 1 1/8" down, as shown. (This may take a little practice.)

Step   7 Rotate and make simple arc cuts at 45 degrees three more times, as in step 7.

Step   8 Set the saw table top back to 0 degrees.

Step   9 Make a half-round radius cut into the center, as shown.

Step 10 Rotate the board and make half round radius cuts three more times until the tulip is free. Be careful in making the last two cuts. Keep your fingers away from the blade.

Step 11 Drill a 1/8"-diameter hole, approximately 1/2" deep, into the bottom of the tulip.

Step 12 Cut 1/8"-diameter dowel to length.

Step 13 Glue the dowel to the tulip and paint it to suit.

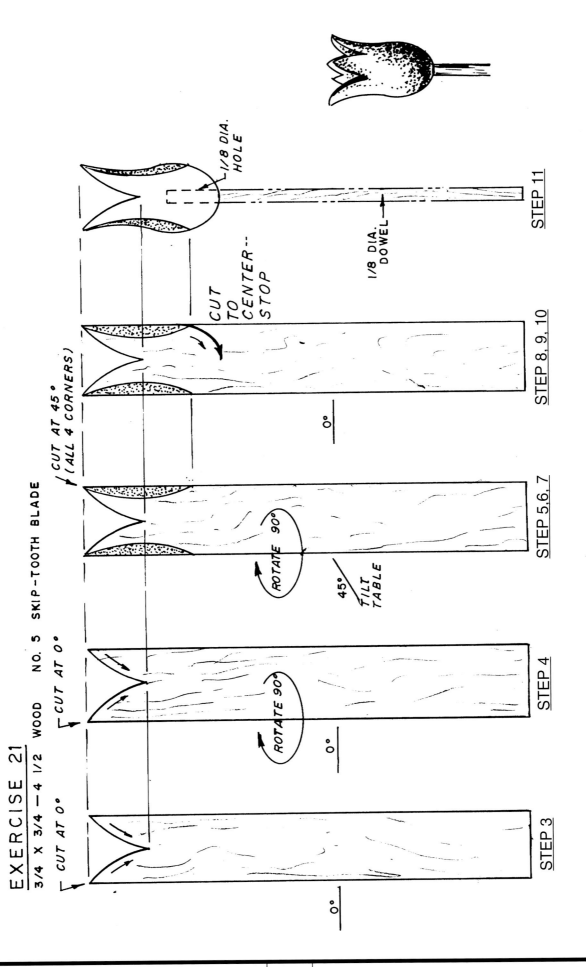

EXERCISE 21

3/4 X 3/4 — 4 1/2 WOOD   NO. 5   SKIP-TOOTH BLADE

CUT AT 0°

CUT AT 0°

CUT AT 45° (ALL 4 CORNERS)

CUT TO CENTER-- STOP

1/8 DIA. HOLE

1/8 DIA. DOWEL

STEP 11

STEP 8, 9, 10

ROTATE 90°

45° TILT TABLE

STEP 5, 6, 7

ROTATE 90°

STEP 4

STEP 3

0°

Objective: Two methods for cutting puzzles.

METHOD A

Materials needed:
(1) 3/4" x 4¹/₂" - 7" long
(2) ¹/₈" x 5" - 7" long plywood

Step   1 Make a copy of Practice Exercise 22 A.

Step   2 Paint the top surface of the puzzle. (Painting the bottom of the puzzle is optional).

NOTE: Always paint a puzzle before cutting it out, as it is almost impossible to paint after cutting out.

Step   3 Attach the pattern to the top surface of the puzzle. Attach a clear piece of paper or cardboard to the bottom surface. This will eliminate any burrs on the bottom surface of the puzzle and save you from having to sand the bottom surface after cutting.

Step   4 Stand or sit directly _in front of_ the saw. Relax and take a deep breath.

Step   5 Make the first long horizontal cut all the way across the puzzle.

Step   6 Make all the other long horizontal cuts.

Step   7 Tape all the horizontal strips back together using ³/₄"-wide masking tape.

Step   8 Make all the vertical cuts.

Step   9 Remove the tape, the pattern and the bottom paper.

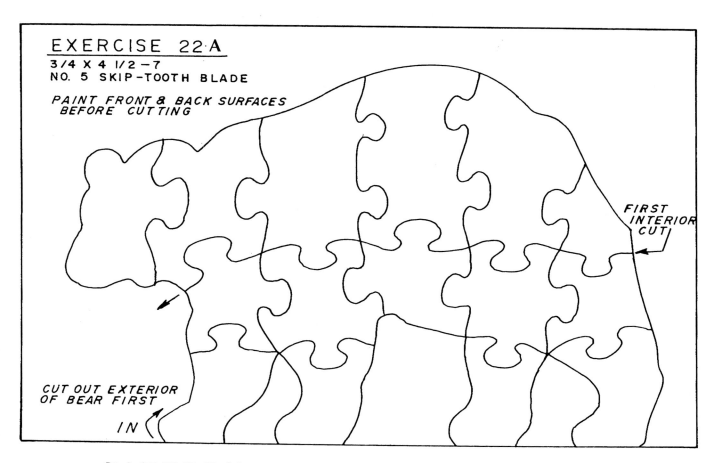

EXERCISE 22·A
3/4 X 4 1/2 —7
NO. 5 SKIP-TOOTH BLADE

PAINT FRONT & BACK SURFACES
BEFORE CUTTING

FIRST
INTERIOR
CUT

CUT OUT EXTERIOR
OF BEAR FIRST

IN

PATTERN

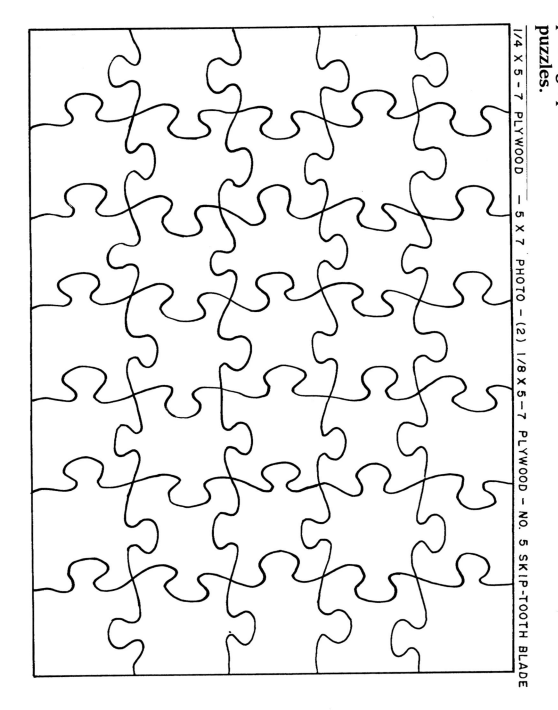

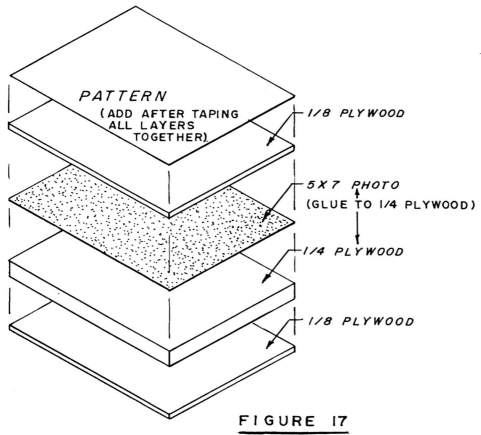

PATTERN
(ADD AFTER TAPING
ALL LAYERS
TOGETHER)

— 1/8 PLYWOOD

— 5 X 7 PHOTO

(GLUE TO 1/4 PLYWOOD)

— 1/4 PLYWOOD

— 1/8 PLYWOOD

FIGURE 17

METHOD B

Materials needed:
(2) 1/4" x 5" x 7" long plywood
(1) 5"x 7" photograph
(1) 1/4" x 5" x 7" long wood
Contact cement
#5 skip tooth blade

Step 1 Make a copy of Practice Exercise 22B (page 76).

Step 2 Cut wood to 5" x 7" and sand all edges.

Step 3 Glue pattern to one of the 1/8" thick pieces of plywood.

Step 4 Apply a coat of adhesive spray to back of 5" x 7" photograph and let dry. Apply a coat of adhesive spray to the top surface of the 1/4" thick piece of plywood and let dry.

Step 5 Apply photograph to 1/4" thick plywood and apply pressure or weight to the pieces to ensure a good bonding. Let sit overnight.

Step 6 Sand all four edges lightly.

Step 7 Make a sandwich of the parts as shown in Step 17 and tape around all four edges. (Refer to page 38, "Stack cutting using the tape method.")

Step 8 Stand or sit directly in front of the saw. Relax and take a deep breath.

Step 9 Make the first long horizontal cut all the way across the puzzle.

Step 10 Make all the other long horizontal cuts.

Step 11 Tape all the horizontal strips back together using 1/8"wide tape.

Step 12 Assemble the puzzle as you make the final cuts.

Note: Try cutting two or three puzzles at a time.

Objective: **To practice using relief cutting to make raised or indented letters. This technique can be used for signs or name tags.**

Materials needed:
(1) $3/4$" x $43/4$" - $67/8$" long piece of pine
#3 skip tooth blade
$1/32$" diameter drill

Step   1 Make a copy of Practice Exercise 23. Cut the wood to size.

Step   2 Attach the pattern (letters) to the wood.

Step   3 Refer to your Relief Cutting Blade/Angle Tester made in Practice Exercise 14 to determine how far you want your letters to extend <u>in</u> or <u>out</u>. In this example, we will make <u>raised</u> letters extending <u>out</u> about $1/4$" or so. Tilt the table, *left side down,* to the angle needed to get letters to extend $1/4$".

Note: To produce relief cutting letters you must cut clockwise and counter-clockwise to get the center areas of A, B, D, O, P, Q and R to either stand out or indent in.

Step   4 Drill small diameter starter holes where indicated.

Step   5 Stand or sit directly *in front of* the saw. Relax and take a deep breath.

Step   6 Make all of the interior cuts of A, B, D, O, P, Q and R first. <u>Important</u>: Cut in the direction noted. Make all of the cuts by making sharp turns at every point. Do not "loop."

Step   7 Now make the exterior cuts.
Step   8 Push all interior areas of the letters A, B, D, O, P, Q and R <u>in</u> as far as they will go.

Step   9 Push all the letters <u>out</u> as far as they will go.

NOTE: Most of the letters should extend <u>in</u> or <u>out</u> about the same amount. If not adjust each so that they all extend <u>in</u> or <u>out</u> the same way.

Step 10 Glue in place from the *back.* A dot of glue here and there should suffice.

Step 11 Finish to suit.

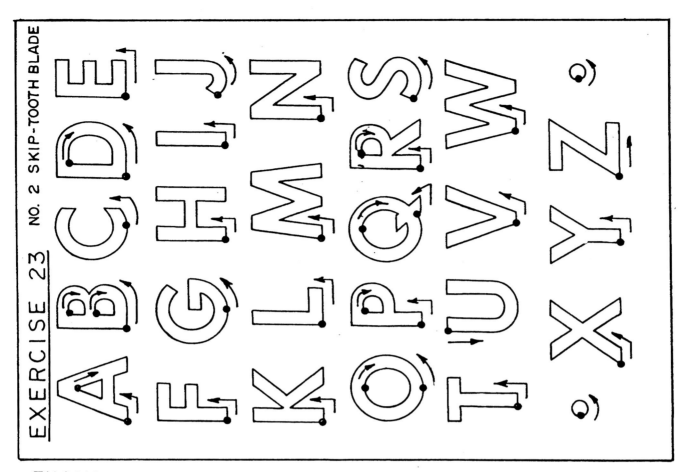

PATTERN

EXAMPLE

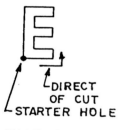

DIRECT
OF CUT
STARTER HOLE

TILT TABLE
LEFT SIDE DOWN

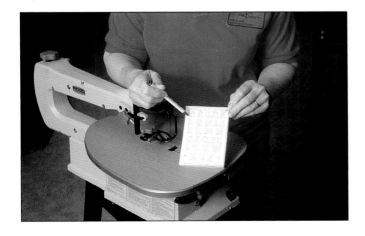

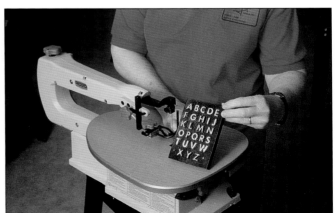

Objective: To practice segmentation, a simplified version of Intarsia.

Materials needed:
(1) ¹/₂" x 7¹/₄" x 7¹/₄" piece of wood
(1) ¹/₈" x 7¹/₄" x 7¹/₄" piece of plywood
Router with ¹/₈" radius round over bit
#5 skip tooth blade
¹/₃₂"-diameter drill

Step   1   Make a copy of Practice Exercise 24 — attach the pattern to the wood.

Note: Segmentation is similar to a field of scrolling called Intarsia. Intarsia incorporates various kinds of woods and/or grain directions to achieve different effects. Most pieces in Intarsia are stained or left natural. The segmentation technique uses one piece of wood cut into small segments. The edges of each segment are rounded slightly and each segment is usually painted a different color.

Step   2   Make the exterior cuts, then cut all the segment pieces. Keep all the pieces in order.

Step   3   Drill starter holes for the eye and pupil. Cut out.

Step   4   Using a router and ¹/₈"-radius round-over bit with a follower, round all of the top edges of each segment piece. (If you do not have a router, simply sand the edges.)

Step   5   Cut out the ¹/₈" backing board as indicated on the pattern.

Step   6   Paint each piece (top and edges only—not the back surface) as indicated. Use a water-based, quick-drying paint. Paint the backing board to suit.

Step   7   Glue the pieces to the backing board. Note that the project will extend over the backing board by ¹/₁₆" to ¹/₈" or so, all around.

Step   8   Apply a clear, water-based varnish to the entire surface. Add a hanger to suit (optional).

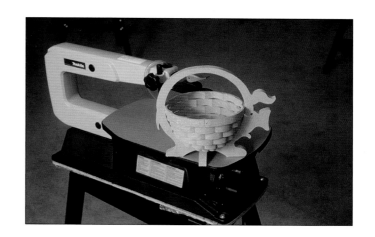

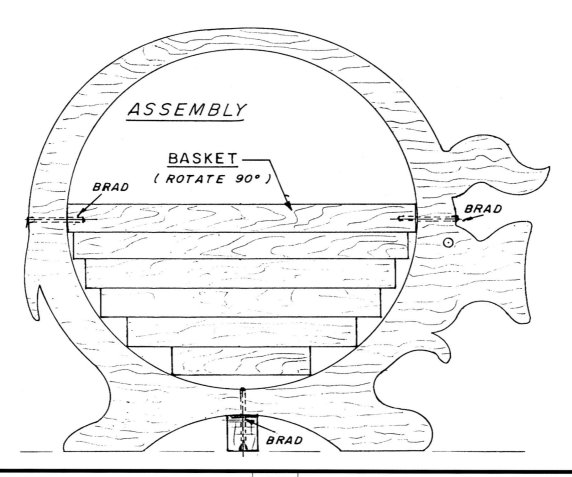

ASSEMBLY

BASKET
(ROTATE 90°)

BRAD

BRAD

BRAD

APPENDIX

This is a list of various scroll saw-related suppliers for your reference. These are the ones we know of at this time. As you become more familiar with scrolling, you will discover others through scroll saw picnics, magazine ads and fellow scrollers.

Call or write them for their catalog. Tell them we sent you.

SCROLL SAWS/ACCESSORIES

Delta
Delta International Machinery
(800) 438-2486

DeWalt (Black & Decker)
(800) 433-9258

Dremel
(800) 437-3635

Eclipse
(804) 779-2478

Excalibur
Sommerville Design
(800) 357-4118

Seyco (Excalibur)
(800) 462-3353

Treeline (Excalibur)
(800) 598-2743

Grizzly Industrial
(800) 541-5537

Hegner
(800) 727-6553

Makita
(800) 462-5482

Powermatic
(800) 248-0144

Pro-Tech Power
(800) 888-6603

Proxxon
(866) 776-9832

PS Wood Machine
PS Machinery, Inc.
(800) 939-4414

RBI
RBIndustries
(800) 487-2623
Rigid
Emerson Tool
(800) 325-1184

Ryobi Power Tools
(800) 525-2579

Shopsmith
(800) 543-7586

Tradesman
(800) 243-5114

SCROLL SAW BOOKS, PATTERNS AND HARDWARE SUPPLIERS

Armor Crafts (Hardware)
PO Box 445
East Northport, NY 11731
(800) 292-8296

Cherry Tree Toys, Inc. (Hardware)
PO Box 369
Belmont, OH 43718
(800) 848-4363
*Inquire about their "Insiders' Club."

Fox Chapel Publishing Co., Inc.
(Books and Magazines)
1970 Broad St.
East Petersburg, PA 17520
(717) 560–4703
www.foxchapelpublishing.com

Klockit Co. (Clocks)
PO box 636
Lake Geneva, WI 53147-0636
(800) 556-2548

Mike's Workshop, Inc. (Blades)
Flying Dutchman Blades
PO Box 107
Brandon, SD 57005
(605) 582–6732

National Artcraft Co. (Hardware)
7996 Darrow Rd.
Twinsburg, OH 44087
(888) 937-2723

P&D Designs (Patterns and Plans)
PO Box 410
Ascutney, VT 05030
(802) 674–6059
http://scrollsawpatternscenter.com

Penn State Industries (Hardware)
2850 Comly Rd.
Philadelphia, PA 19154
(800) 377-7297
The Olson Saw Company (Blades)
16 Stony Hill Rd.
Bethel, CT 06801

Scroll Saw Workshop Magazine
1970 Broad St.
East Petersburg, PA 17520
(888) 840–8590
www.scrollsawer.com

Sloan's Woodshop (Hardware)
3453 Callis Rd.
Lebanon, TN 37090
(888) 615-9663
http://members.aol.com/scroll-wood/homepage/index.htm

Steebar Corp. (Clocks)
PO Box 980
Andover, NJ 07821-0980
(973) 383-1026

Turncraft Clocks, Inc. (Clocks)
PO box 100
Mound, MN 55364-0100

Time Savers (Clocks)
Box 12700
Scottsdale, AZ 85267
(800) 552–1520

ARM LIFT FOR DEWALT – EXCALIBUR ONLY

Jim Dandy Products, Inc. *(Spring operated)*
1695 Boundry Rd.
Downers Grove, IL 60516
(800) 522-4717

Paul Revere *(Foot operated)*
PO Box 5195
Navarre, FL 32566
(850) 939-3968

Seyco *(Excalibur only)*
(800) 462-3353

SCROLL SAW MAGAZINES, NEWSLETTERS AND MUSEUMS

Billy Clock Museum
PO Box 258
Spillville, IA 52168
(319) 356-3569

Creative Woodworks and Crafts
(Magazine)
PO Box 518
Mt. Morris, IL 61054
(800) 877-5527

INSTRUCTIONAL VIDEOS

For those of you who cannot get to a basic scroll saw seminar, consider purchasing a video to get started. These videos demonstrate some of the slightly advanced, unique things the scroll saw can do, such as stack cutting, compound cutting (3-D) and relief cutting.

Advanced Scroll Sawing I
with Alex Snodgrass
Purchase from P.S. Wood Machines
10 Downing St.-Suite 3
Library, PA 15129
(800)-939-4414

Intarsia
with Judy Gale Roberts and
Jerry Booher
Fox Chapel Publishing
1970 Broad St.
East Petersburg, PA 17520
(800) 457-9112

Learning To Use Your Scroll Saw
with Joanne Lockwood
Purchase from Advanced
Machinery Imports, Ltd.
PO Box 312
New Castle, DE 19720-0312
(800) 220-4264

Scroll Saw Projects
with Mark Berner
Purchase from Walnut Creek
Woodworking Supply, Co.
3601 West Harry
Wichita, KS 67200
(800) 942-0553

Scroll Sawing Basics-How To Turn
Them Into Cash
with Rick and Karen Longabaugh
Purchase from The Berry Basket
PO Box 925
Centralia, WA 98531
(800) 206-9009

THIN WOOD SUPPLIERS

Blue Ox Brand
PO Box 715
Kenmore, NY 14217
(800) 758-0950

Croffwood Mills
RD #1 Box 14C
Driftwood, PA 15832
(814) 546-2532

D & D Woodcrafts
RR 3 Box 3066
Saylorburg, PA 18353
(610) 381-2286

D. J. Hardwoods
317 Nebraska Ave.
Columbia, MO 65201
(800) 514-3449

Good Hope Hardwoods
1627 New London Rd.
Landenberg, PA 19350
(610) 274-8842

Groff and Hearne Lumber
858 Scotland Rd.
Quarryville, PA 17566
(800) 342-0001

Hartford Woodworks
Box 41B
Blaine, ME 04734
(207) 425-2911

Heritage Building Specialties
205 N. Cascade
Fergus Falls, MN 56537
(800) 524-4184

Memphis Hardwood Lumber
6535 Church St.
Memphis, NY 13112
(800) 286-3949

Sloan's Woodshop
3453 Callis Rd.
Lebanon, TN 37090
(615) 435-2222

Tuckaway Timber Co.
Lyme, NH 03768
(603) 795-4534

West Friendship Hardwood
PO Box 103
West Friendship, MD 21794
(410) 489-9236

Willard Brothers
300 Basin Rd.
Trenton, NJ 08619

Woods of The World
867 Rt. 12
Westmoreland Park
Westmoreland, NH 03467
(603) 352-8000

PLYWOOD SUPPLIERS

Boulter Plywood Corp.
24 Broadway
Somerville, MA 02145

Constantine
2050 Eastchester Rd.
Bronx, NY 10461

Memphis Hardwood Lumber
6535 Church St.
Memphis, NY 13112
(800) 286-3949

RBI's Lumber Yard
RBIndustries
PO Box 369
Harrisonville, MO 64701

Sloan's Woodshop
5543 Edmondson Pike Box 61
Nashville, TN 37211
(615)831-0176

SCROLL SAW PICNICS

A great way to learn all about
scrolling is to attend the various
scroll saw picnics all around the
country.
Contact SCROLL SAW ASSOCIA-
TION OF THE WORLD for dates and
locations.

Scroll Saw Association of the World
610 Daisy Lane
Round Lake Beach, IL 60073-2219
(847) 546-1319 Fax: (847) 546-
1352

CHAT ROOMS

Intarsia Group —
http://groups.yahoo.com/group/in
tarsiawoodwork/

Ontario, Canada Group —
http://ca.groups.yahoo.com/group
.ontarioscrollers/

Australian Group —
http://au.groups.yahoo.com/group
/ozscrollsaw/

Scrollsaw Association of the World
Chapter Group —
http://groups.yahoolcom/group/sa
wchapteronline/

Lots of Clocks Group —
http://groups.yahoo.com/group/sc
rollsawclocks/

The First and Oldest Scroll Saw
Group —
http://groups.yahoo.com/group/sc
rollsawing/

The Art of Scrolling Group —
hppt://groups.yahoo.com/group/s
crollsawingart/